Guest-edited by
Samantha Hardingham

SERIOUS FUN

THE ARTY-TECTURE OF WILL ALSOP

**About the
Guest-Editor**

5

Samantha Hardingham

Introduction

6

On the Visible
Spectrum

Samantha Hardingham

**Notes on a 20-Year
Partnership**

14

Challenging Architecture
and Each Other

John Lyall

Where There's a Will …

22

Peter Cook

A Second Course in
Architecture

30

Samantha Hardingham

Willie Wonky and the
Arty-tecture Factory

38

Nigel Coates

Will Power

46

Paul Finch

Yes, This Is
Architecture

54

Neil Thomas

Forty B&H and
a Pork Pie

62

My Dad the Architect

Ollie Alsop

Collaboration and
Friendship, Art
and Architecture

70

Will McLean

ISSN 0003-8504   ISBN 978 1119 833932

Guest-edited by **Samantha Hardingham**

78

Building Knowledge   102
Reflections on
Peckham Library

Thomas Aquilina

Back to His Roots   110
aLL Design – the Legacy of
an All-inclusive Architect

Marcos Rosello

'Where so much
architecture is focused
on known targets –
the canon if you will –
Alsop had his sights on
the unknowns, or what
he called "creative
noise" and the ability
"to go beyond what
he knows".'

— **Samantha Hardingham**

Seeing Things   78
Differently
Painting, the Object and the
Art of Conversation

Clare Hamman

The WillS of Words   86
An Alsop Mediagraphy

Mark Garcia

Art of the Impossible   94
A Posthumous Supercrit

Kester Rattenbury

From Another Perspective   118

Five Cigarettes
or Seven?

Neil Spiller

Contributors   126

Editorial Offices
John Wiley & Sons
9600 Garsington Road
Oxford
OX4 2DQ

T +44 (0)18 6577 6868

Editor
Neil Spiller

Managing Editor
Caroline Ellerby
Caroline Ellerby Publishing

Freelance Contributing Editor
Abigail Grater

Publisher
Todd Green

Art Direction + Design
Christian Küsters +
Mihaela Mincheva
CHK Design

Production Editor
Elizabeth Gongde

Prepress
Artmedia, London

Printed in the United Kingdom
by Hobbs the Printers Ltd

Front cover
Top left: Alsop Architects,
Sharp Centre for Design,
Ontario College of Art & Design
(OCAD), Toronto, Canada, 2004.
© Richard Johnson

Clockwise from top right:
Will Alsop, *Yubei*, 2016; Will
Alsop, *Spiral*, 2015; aLL Design,
Shanghai International Cruise
Terminal 'Gao Yang', Shanghai,
China, 2010. © aLL Design

Inside front cover
Will Alsop, *Untitled*, 1999.
Image courtesy of the Marco
Goldschmied Foundation MGF,
photo Clare Hamman

Δ	ARCHITECTURAL DESIGN		
September/October		Volume	Issue
2022		92	05
	WILEY.COM		

Acknowledgement
Samantha Hardingham
and Neil Spiller would like
to thank Sheila Alsop for
her enthusiastic support
for the preparation of
this issue, and Dorotea
Petrucci for her dedicated
assistance in sourcing
materials.

Journal Customer Services
For ordering information,
claims and any enquiry
concerning your journal
subscription please go to
www.wileycustomerhelp
.com/ask or contact your
nearest office.

Americas
E: cs-journals@wiley.com
T: +1 877 762 2974

**Europe, Middle East
and Africa**
E: cs-journals@wiley.com
T: +44 (0)1865 778 315

Asia Pacific
E: cs-journals@wiley.com
T: +65 6511 8000

Japan (for Japanese-
speaking support)
E: cs-japan@wiley.com
T: +65 6511 8010

Visit our Online Customer
Help available in 7 languages
at www.wileycustomerhelp
.com/ask

Print ISSN: 0003-8504
Online ISSN: 1554-2769

Prices are for six issues
and include postage
and handling charges.
Individual-rate subscriptions
must be paid by personal
cheque or credit card.
Individual-rate subscriptions
may not be resold or
used as library copies.

All prices are subject to
change without notice.

Identification Statement
Periodicals Postage paid
at Rahway, NJ 07065.
Air freight and mailing in
the USA by Mercury Media
Processing, 1850 Elizabeth
Avenue, Suite C, Rahway,
NJ 07065, USA.

USA Postmaster
Please send address changes
to *Architectural Design*,
John Wiley & Sons Inc.,
c/o The Sheridan Press,
PO Box 465, Hanover,
PA 17331, USA.

Subscribe to Δ
Δ is published bimonthly
and is available to purchase
on both a subscription basis
and as individual volumes
at the following prices.

Prices
Individual copies:
£29.99 / US$45.00
Individual issues on
Δ App for iPad:
£9.99 / US$13.99
Mailing fees for print
may apply

Annual Subscription Rates
Student: £97 / US$151
print only
Personal: £151 / US$236
print and iPad access
Institutional: £357 / US$666
online only
Institutional: £373 / US$695
print only
Institutional: £401 / US$748
print and online

6-issue subscription
on Δ App for iPad:
£44.99 / US$64.99

Samantha Hardingham is an independent designer, writer, curator and scholar in the field of experimental architectural practice. Her work across all disciplines focuses on developing new and relevant formats whether for talks, publications or building proposals, each responding to the context with the aim of engaging new audiences. She studied at the Architectural Association (AA) in London (1987–93). Having been introduced to the late Will Alsop by a mutual friend, he gave her some advice on preparing a portfolio for the school and encouraged her to apply. She later led a design unit there for almost 10 years with Archigram member David Greene, who had been Will's tutor at the AA in the 1970s. The unit developed a methodology of search (not research) and 'film-as-sketchbook' to generate time-based design responses as a by-product of an internet-based culture. She was also the school's Interim Director from 2017 to 2018.

During a five-year appointment as a senior research fellow in the Experimental Practice Research Group at the University of Westminster (2003–08), she devised and launched the Supercrit series of events and publications with colleague Kester Rattenbury. Following a short period in design practice, developing new experiential entertainment formats, she is currently Academic Director of the London School of Architecture (LSA). The school was founded in 2012 as a new model of postgraduate architectural education that seeks to widen access and participation across all disciplines that make the built environment, and to challenge related teaching methodologies.

Her publications include several editions of *London: A Guide to Recent Architecture* and *England: A Guide to Recent Architecture* that launched the innovative ellipsis guidebook series in 1994, as well as *Cedric Price Opera* (Wiley, 2003) and *Cedric Price Retriever* (INIVA, 2005).

Her most notable work is a 10-year research project that became the two-volume *Cedric Price Works 1954–2003: A Forward-Minded Retrospective* (AA Publications/ Canadian Centre for Architecture, 2016) and led to a number of associated exhibitions including commissions for the AA (London, 2012), Bureau-Europa national architecture museum (Maastricht, 2014) and the Venice Architecture Biennale (2016). 🗅

On the Visible Spectrum

Welcome to the extraordinarily colourful life and work of British architect Will Alsop (1947–2018). His architecture was aimed at allowing 'beautiful resolutions to emerge truthfully from the actual condition of our towns and cities'[1] and replacing 'a little misery in the world with a little joy and delight', and he did this with style and showmanship – with what he called 'creative noise'. Alsop consistently worked around, over and above and beyond what the conventions of the architectural canon could chart.[2] In the words of his hero, English architect Cedric Price (1934–2003), he engaged in the serious fun of 'aiming to miss'.[3] Price used the following analogy in a talk to assembled architects in 1975 to describe the activity of design as he saw it: 'If you try and fire in a fairground between moving ducks you are far less interested in the size of the ducks [than] you are in the speed of them. You are still watching the target. You are aiming to miss.'[4] He demanded that design take on the mess, the mistakes and perceptibly inadequate, imperfect conditions and unwanted by-products of a situation: calculating waste, usefulness of shadows, aspirations for short-term occupancy and similarly unknown quantities. Serious fun is the practice of designing for these conditions that are approximate and that change over time.

SMC Alsop,
Westside Sales Centre,
Toronto, Canada,
2008

An initial digital concept drawing-cum-collage explores layers of primary structure and an envelope with irregular-shaped openings that is then developed across sketch models and full-scale building cassettes.

Price answered these questions in his own design practice by thinking about the processes of construction, engaging phased design solutions, and building in obsolescence and multiple targets so clients had the capacity to change their minds in time. The approach required a wholesale questioning of all aspects of a brief, starting with the client's intentions for seeking an architect in the first place.

Alsop would have attended this talk – he was a young architect embarking on his career, and was working for Price, so it is not disingenuous to assume the idea clearly made a big impression and something of the thinking rubbed off. Alsop went on to refine a method over 50 years that took on the part about questioning what the client thinks they want in their architect and making sure that he was included in the answer – aiming to miss one target and in the process hitting many more. Whilst Price designed a structure and framework – let's call it 'how to source a few well-chosen ingredients and prepare a recipe for a hearty dish to be assembled as and when required' – Alsop chose to design the ultimate kitchen in which to collectively produce a variety of dishes for any and all to feast on. It says much about their generational differences and the contexts in which they were both practising.

Alsop Architects,
Studio 3,
Battersea, London,
2003

Studio 3 was the creative department of Alsop's architectural studio when it was based in Battersea Bridge Road. Here graphic designer Mark Boyce, a member of the studio, experiments with projection overlays of drawings and paintings onto wall-size book page layouts.

Both have been labelled mavericks. Price was comfortable with calling himself whatever he liked – he saw this as his right, and his alone – but rejected the imposition, considering it a slur on his intellect and architectural competencies. Alsop, on the other hand, embraced it as giving him permission to think bigger and experiment freely to change minds and enliven cities. He developed the kind of continuous and robust process of design experimentation required to help others make sense of their own noise, achieving this through drawing, talking, presenting, modelling, teaching, writing, performing, designing and his own distinct method of painting. Neither Price nor Alsop were aiming to please and, as such, their lives and their architecture have infuriated and delighted many.

The contributions in this issue seek to ensure that Alsop remains on the visible spectrum of architectural discourse as amiable agent provocateur, and that his buildings are remembered as flashes of brilliance in an otherwise overwhelmingly subdued built environment. They are written by close friends and collaborators, with one or two exceptions where the writers have sought out first-hand material and accounts. Readers may fear the issue lacks criticality in this respect, but Alsop was no stranger to criticism during his lifetime. He is not long gone from this world, so this slim volume makes a moment of noisy silence, before history marches on to cut and shape future narratives.

On Learning

Alsop's career and philosophy of architecture was shaped by his education and those he encountered in schools and studios of art and architecture, most crucially the Architectural

SMC Alsop,
Façade treatment
for an apartment/
gallery block in
Toronto, Canada,
2008

Detail from one of a series of physical sketch models made to test different materials and the joining of an undulating surface with irregular-shaped openings. This model was made for a proposal to be sited on the same street as the Westside Sales Centre.

SMC Alsop,
Westside Sales Centre,
Toronto, Canada,
2008

Will Alsop poses in front of the completed Westside Sales Centre. Prefabricated timber cassettes make up the cladding, incorporating the irregular-shaped openings as developed out of earlier study models.

Association (AA) in London (1969–73) with some years after engaged in tutoring there, and then in the offices of Cedric Price Architects (1973–77) as set out in my own article in this issue, 'A Second Course in Architecture'. John Lyall's recollections of a time spent experimenting and learning at the AA provides considerable insight into a pluralistic training shared under the influence of Tony Dugdale, Keith Critchlow, Archigram, Price and Buckminster Fuller, amongst others. A student partnership, under the guise of Match then Multimatch, was formalised as Alsop & Lyall in 1980. Peter Cook, ringmaster of the London (and now global) architectural scene since the 1960s, creates a vivid invocation of the atmosphere that coincided with Alsop's early career years as one of creative and quick-witted mischief. Cook deftly sketches out a portrait of Will that touches on all his dimensions, from optimistic and open-minded educator to sagely confident and rakish architect/entertainer. Cook's pace and choice of words pop along to the beat of those groovy times. This tune is also played out by Nigel Coates who extends a characterisation of Alsop through a description of his teaching methods in schools of architecture. In 'Willie Wonky and the Arty-tecture Factory', Coates depicts the architect as a great disrupter who liked a work-in and threw himself and everyone else into the deep end. In Alsop's hands it was a means, as Coates puts it, to 'nurture audacity' amongst his student audiences in order to 'think bigger, brighter and more courageously'. Coates' title sums up so much of Alsop's activity and method, so it seemed fitting to borrow it for the title of this issue too.

On Practising

Alsop's practices and partnerships took many forms and as such the trajectory was not always straightforward. Over the course of his career his practice adapted seven times: Alsop & Lyall became Alsop, Lyall & Störmer in 1990 (renamed to incorporate the German partner Jan Störmer), Alsop & Störmer from 1991 to 2000, Alsop Architects from 2000 to 2006, SMC Alsop from 2006 to 2009, Will Alsop at RMJM from 2009 to 2011, and finally aLL Design in 2011, which continues today. These changes are charted in this issue alongside the production of projects and buildings by editor and architectural journalist Paul Finch, who offers the perspective of one who closely followed Alsop's entire career through the pages of architectural magazines. He takes us on a fly-through tour of all the greatest hits, leaving us aghast at the number of landmark buildings built and that have precipitated social, economic and political change in the cities in which they have landed.

Structural engineer Neil Thomas was a collaborator on the Cardiff Bay Visitor Centre in Wales (1990), one of the first projects to bring the practice Alsop, Lyall & Störmer considerable public exposure. Thomas describes in his article how their working time together was a course of 'unexpected exploration' and acknowledges the extremes to which Alsop was able, and he himself was willing, to push both conceptual and technical architectural boundaries. Alsop was prolific, never holding on to one idea for too long – this was profound for Thomas and something that he continues to deploy in his own work in order to liberate design ideas.

Alsop's son, Ollie, offers a uniquely professional and personal account of his father's tics and design habits that again track this chronology (albeit starting from 1977 on his arrival into the world). For him, the early years of practice are a bit of a blur, but the neatly arranged drawing implements set out each day on the breakfast table are still crystal clear. Their later collaborations on films and creating venues were inspired. Ollie recalls with awe, smacked by tragedy, the live televised acceptance speech on winning the Stirling Prize for Peckham Library, London, in 2000, when Alsop took advantage of the platform to take a less than flattering pop at the London Borough of Kensington and Chelsea – 'mortifying at the time … But on reflection, I miss him for his controversy'.

On Painting

Bruce and Will McLean, Clare Hamman and Mark Garcia each take on that other messy subject – painting. Will McLean was a member of Alsop's office in the 1980s and 1990s and talks to his father, artist Bruce McLean, about his 40-year-long friendship and collaboration with Alsop. He is insistent and understated about their working method, as one which was not about the pursuit of making art for art's sake but rather one of testing and re-testing ideas that was alive, direct, visceral and often beautiful. Will McLean reflects on a collaborative practice that was highly spirited, and where the process of painting sat firmly in relation to all the subsequent stages of bringing about an architectural design, from their interpretation in models to conjuring spatial atmospheres. Hamman reinforces this perspective, describing how the paintings are foundational for each architectural project, serving to harness an atmosphere or essential characteristics. Garcia focuses on Alsop's words. These appeared in paintings and 'the multi media/transmedia nature of his outputs, where often word, art, architecture, text and image were blurred into total, immersive spaces of ideas', but they also found their way into more conventional communications such as articles, talks, TV presentations and film scripts.

opposite top: Physical sketch models were developed directly from paintings and drawings. The model, with a similar degree of immediacy to the paintings, starts to investigate rudimentary structure and skin.

opposite bottom: A digital model is developed from the physical sketch model to start to rationalise a system of structural panels for the main building envelope.

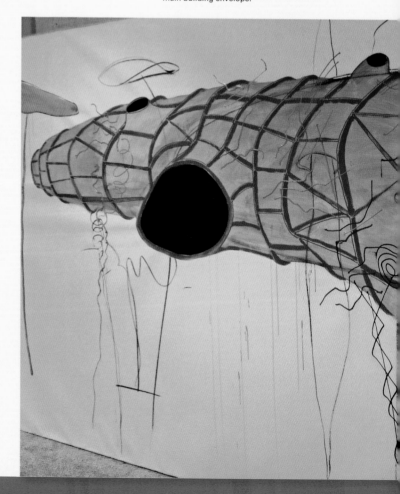

Will Alsop at RMJM, Museum proposal, Edessa, Greece, 2009

Wall-sized painted sketches for a proposal for a museum located over an archaeological site. Alsop used these large paintings and drawings as a means to explore different aspects of an architectural project – in this instance, the development of an anthropomorphic architectural form.

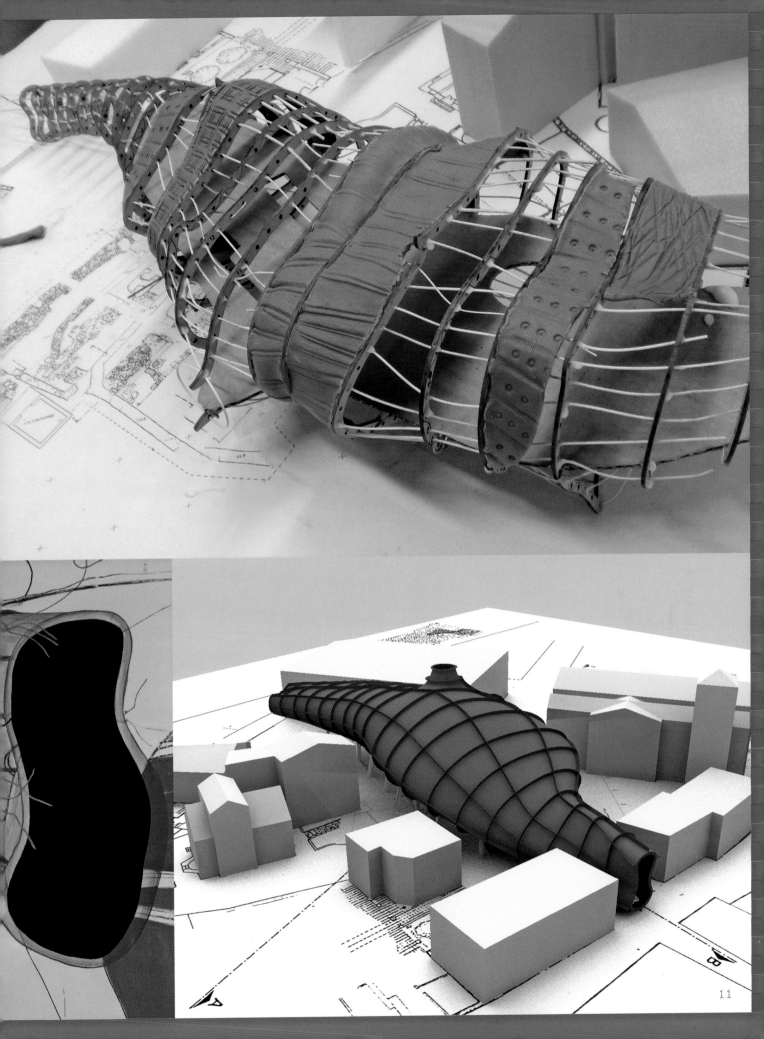

A conceptual photomontage competition entry for a seaside masterplan shows a cigarette lighter held up to serve as a scale model of the building proposal amongst other landscape interventions. Alsop is reported to have based the earlier Cardiff Bay Visitor Centre (1990) on an oval-shaped Bic cigarette lighter.

Alsop's buildings and artworks are as contentious as they have been highly acclaimed, but never fail to amaze and inspire

On Reflection

The final three articles of the issue turn away from the architect figure and towards his architecture to offer reflections on some key projects. Kester Rattenbury reports on the Supercrit #8 event that took place at the University of Westminster in 2018 to chart the development and delivery of the Hôtel du Département des Bouches-du-Rhône ('Le Grand Bleu') governmental building in Marseille, France (1994). Members of the design team recall the highs and lows of the competition and construction work and offer a well-rounded portrayal of this groundbreaking project. Similarly, Thomas Aquilina, the youngest contributor and the only one not to have met Alsop directly, does spatial justice to Peckham Library in a short film made with his architectural group Afterparti for the Architecture Foundation (2022). In the film, Aquilina and team speak to structural engineer Hanif Kara from AKT II, project architect Christophe Egret and Tszwai So of Spheron Architects who are working on a current redesign for the public square in front of the building. The film brings out the critical role that libraries play in making our cities and how they empower communities to build knowledge of and for themselves, and for future residents.

On Time

The last word goes to Marcos Rosello who currently leads aLL Design. He describes the central tenets of the practice and how as a team they try to uphold aspects of Alsop's design ethos: to 'make life better' for people and places, to 'knock nothing down' because memories and a sense of place enhance an existing grain, and to testbed ideas with communities and collaboration.

Many of Alsop's built projects caused big shifts in thinking about ways for citizens to perceive, occupy and enjoy their cities. He believed deeply in the power of active participation, for clients to explore their architectural ideas, involving them in workshops and the making of films and huge paintings to help them to see and better understand what design could do for them. His buildings and artworks are as contentious as they have been highly acclaimed, but never fail to amaze and inspire. They show a way forward for a new generation of architects who, let's face it, could use a little joy given the last couple of years of confinement, experiencing life through a screen only. This 𝗗 aims to reignite some interactive, messy, energetic creative collisions and offers a plethora of ways to go about it. 𝗗

Notes

1. Tom Porter, *Will Alsop: The Noise*, Routledge (New York), 2011, p 154.
2. *Ibid*, p 33.
3. Cedric Price, *Aiming to Miss*, 20 November 1975 – the concluding part of a three-part lecture series delivered at Art Net: https://www.youtube.com/watch?v=IzJ4Hb7Wi7Y.
4. *Ibid*.

Notes on a 20-Year Partnership

Challenging Architecture and Each Other

John Lyall

John Lyall,
The Fold Out Story,
London,
1969

The distinctly personalised cover of Lyall's First Year portfolio for a group
project (with Mikhail Mandrigin and others) to design and build a structure
for the homeless charity Shelter. The graphic style is a direct reflection of
the real delight that Lyall and fellow students convey when speaking about
the project and as recorded inside the book in picture captions.

Alsop's first business partner of two decades, **John Lyall** describes their formative years as students at the Architectural Association in London, the influence of various members of Archigram, and sharing a house in Southeast London's not-so-salubrious Ladywell district. He recounts a world of music gigs, designing events and parties, and the offices they worked for as young architects before forming their fledgling practice in the 1970s.

It was September 1968, and I was nervously attending the First Year's introduction day at the Architectural Association (AA) School of Architecture in London. Students had come from all over the globe – worldly wise with wide-ranging experiences: quite a few had worked already, like Rem Koolhaas (he had been a journalist in the Netherlands); some had already completed a degree elsewhere. And there stood Will Alsop clutching a drawing board and a T-square; like he knew how to use them! The AA Principal (as the role was then called) John Lloyd gave a stirring speech about how AA students could change the world with an architectural education. There was a lot of youthful optimism in the UK at the time. He also warned us that the top 10 per cent of students would be 'misfits' in the profession. As one of that new group of students, I for one wished to join that select band.

Experimenting and Learning at the AA

Architect and great teacher Tony Dugdale was in charge of the First Year, and he made it clear very quickly that architecture was not just about designing buildings, but invention, understanding how systems worked, and using technologies freely to solve problems and meet challenges. The course was loosely based on an eclectic combination of the pedagogical principles of Germany's Bauhaus (founded 1919) that progressively dissolved the distinction between artists and artisans, with an indulgence in what was happening in the state-of-the-art space programme at Cape Canaveral in Florida at the time, and intense absorption in the work of polymath Buckminster Fuller (1895–1983), under the stewardship of artist and author on pattern and geometry, Keith Critchlow. Equipped with this most pluralistic of influences and expertise, fellow student Mikhail Mandrigin and I designed and built a 15-metre (50-foot) diameter folding geodesic dome for a travelling exhibition for the homeless charity Shelter. Published in London's *Evening Standard* newspaper, it was not a bad start.

That first summer Dugdale recommended me, as a student who could draw, to work for Cedric Price Architects at his offices in Alfred Place, Bloomsbury, just around the corner from the AA. Cedric introduced concepts of indeterminacy and a wide-ranging way of looking at architecture which stayed with me for the rest of my career.

By the Second Year Will and I were sharing a house in Ladywell, Southeast London with another fellow student and kindred spirit, Andrew Munro. We turned the ground floor into an office and precociously created a practice which we called Match. All subsequent student projects were treated as real, live jobs and indeed some were commissioned as our reputations grew. Making and experimenting were key to our activities. The First Year folding dome experience led to a commission for composer and conductor Peter Maxwell Davies, contemporary composer Harrison Birtwistle and chamber music ensemble the Pierrot Players. A large star-shaped aluminium stage structure embraced the performing musicians at the Queen Elizabeth Hall at London's Southbank Centre. The musicians used the star's spikes to suspend odd percussion instruments such as flowerpots and milk bottles. The structure was then recycled with a welded PVC skin for the first Glastonbury Festival in Somerset (1971), where the organisers also asked us to design a shelter from a collection of ex-Royal Air Force parachutes that had been donated, to sleep 200 people – an early air structure! Festivals were a fantastic place to practise our craft; we made event proposals for a 'Futures Festival' in London (1971) and the Isle of Wight Pop Festival (1972).

By the Third and Fourth Years, the 'Match' team moved to rented railway arches in Hungerford Lane under Charing Cross Railway Station. Alvin Boyarsky convened the international architectural 'Summer Session' of 1971 (a series of architectural conventions that he established prior to taking up the role of AA Director later the same year) and appointed Match to organise the closing party at our studio and in the surrounding medieval-looking cobbled streets. It was a memorable and noisy evening of live rock bands, too much wine, and many famous architects gathering from all parts of the world dancing in our street – only to be drenched by buckets of water discharged by the local residents (an interesting mix of prostitutes and labourers) bothered by the noise. This was quite a welcome to the London scene for Alvin.

Our group expanded and was renamed Multimatch, and our tutors were David Greene, Warren Chalk and Ron Herron – all members of the avant-garde Archigram group. Their 'Instant City' philosophy certainly influenced our attitude to changeable, transformative and temporary – very Pricean too. The studio became a preferred gathering place for tutors and fellow students alike. Two particularly significant projects were produced during this time. One was called SINK, which tested us to design for an extreme environment. Will, Andrew and I all took scuba diving lessons and then designed an easily portable chamber for divers to use on the seabed. A full-size prototype using welded latex inflated by air cylinders, and an ingenious

airlock, was erected at the AA. Our tutors and examiners were locked inside while we fed them a recorded narrative through headphones – an unusual way of doing a design review, but they loved it!

The other project that gained much attention was our entry for the international competition for the Centre Pompidou arts centre in Paris (1971). There were 275 entries from all over the world, and we were awarded joint second place for our submerged 'Paris Hills' design which offered Paris a new park as well as a cultural building. The judges' report by Philip Johnson called our design 'childish', but we took it that he meant 'child-like' in the translation from the French.

Notwithstanding our apparent celebrity status as a student group, when it came to assessment examinations the AA would not tolerate a joint submission from three students. Our combined portfolio of collaborative projects dry-mounted on sheets of cloud-shaped aluminium was in the form of a giant matchbox on wheels. This we pushed early one morning up St Martin's Lane from our studio to the AA in Bedford Square, only to be told by the registrar that we had to divide the work up and explain who did what. We eventually passed, but this story continues to be instructive for students working in groups today.

John Lyall,
The Fold Out Story,
London,
1969

A page from Lyall's First Year portfolio showing the final stage of the on-site deployment of the structure which housed exhibition material for the homeless charity Shelter. The highly ambitious 'live' project set a standard for the students from the outset of their architectural education – ready to address all aspects of a design brief from structural and material calculations and their resolution, to the graphic design of accompanying publicity materials.

The Start of Alsop & Lyall and the Riverside Years

Throughout our student years, Will and I had both worked for many different architectural practices during holidays in order to pay our way. After finishing our studies in 1973 I was engaged by the London office of Piano + Rogers, who were also building the Centre Pompidou at the time, and then worked for various firms including a spell in Nebraska in the US helping to shape a new city park in Omaha with Bahr, Vermeer & Haecker Architects and then back in the UK with Rock Townsend in 1979. Meanwhile Will had employment with the theatre architect Roderick Ham and also worked for a period in Cedric Price's offices on the Inter-Action centre (1981).

Our creative relationship was based on positively challenging each other to progress a good concept, whilst individually having different design and technical skills. Small schemes and competitions kept us occupied and provided an education in practice management, how to pursue commissions, and importantly what sort of work we did not wish to end up doing. Richard Rogers's office in Hammersmith, West London, gave us some rent-free space in their old warehouse near Olympia in West Kensington. I worked for that practice by day and did a 'night shift' with Will on our own projects.

The first big break came in 1979, when Rogers recommended us to David Gothard, director of the nearby Riverside Studios. The newly formed arts centre occupied ex-BBC television studios on the Thames riverfront. They wanted to add a bookshop, which we subsequently delivered. It included a mini mobile book display tower that was moved into the foyer during shows and busy event days. It was a low-budget but very striking, almost Japanese-inspired design.

The natural next step for us was to design the masterplan and a commercial development for Riverside Studios which would pay for its expansion and secure its future. The scheme attracted a lot of attention, was publicised widely in both trade and local newspapers, and was politically controversial. It was granted planning permission but sadly never built due to turbulent local politics. In appearance it may have elements that look rather Postmodern, with echoes of some of Aldo Rossi's work – looking back perhaps. Archigram co-founder Peter Cook once referred to us as 'lyrical mechanists', which I guess was a good description at the time.

During this period we had moved into a small studio office given by our clients facing the river and accessed by a spiral staircase. We put on architectural events and exhibitions including a weekend series of talks in 1984 by architects such as Cook, Alison and Peter Smithson, Zaha Hadid, James Gowan (of Stirling and Gowan), Mike Gold and Nigel Coates. We collaborated with resident artists Bruce McLean and Gareth Jones, and 10 years later I worked on dance performances with choreographer Rosemary Butcher whom we had also encountered at Riverside. We were embedded in a rich cultural scene, and designed spaces for the BBC TV studios and Sundance Fitness and Dance Studios in a nearby warehouse (1982). A series of unusual projects followed: a design for a new river pier at Westminster near the Houses of Parliament (placed second in a Greater London Council-run competition), a floating fire station (which was built in 1991 and is still moored near Lambeth Bridge), and an all-steel lifting bridge control centre affectionately called 'The Chicken' (1990) – again built, and which once stood out boldly in the abandoned dockland area of East London but is today dwarfed by a bigger bird, Canary Wharf.

While Will was away teaching in Australia, the city architect of Hamburg in Germany, Professor Egbert Kossak, arrived at our studio to check us out for a big ideas competition for transforming a critical area between the Hauptbahnhof and the Rathaus in the centre of the city. In excelling in this competition against several local German, Austrian and Italian architects we met Jan Störmer, who left his practice me di um in Hamburg and joined us in a cross-channel alliance to undertake future German projects.

Alsop & Lyall,
Bookshop at Riverside Studios,
Hammersmith, London,
1979

The first built work delivered as a partnership was an intervention in a concrete frame, with cross bracing and square, red-stained timber sections for the windows. Some dancers happened to be rehearsing in the studios on the day of the photo shoot so the architects invited them to pose with the building, adding a sense of scale and dynamism to the images.

Alsop & Lyall,
Riverside Studios redevelopment,
London,
1982

John Lyall (second left) and Will Alsop (second right) with their Alsop & Lyall team holding the model for the iconic Riverside Studios development on their Hammersmith terrace.

Alsop, Lyall & Störmer,
Control Centre and
Lifting Bridges,
Canary Wharf, London,
1990

Known as 'The Chicken', the all-steel building (frame and panels) houses the hydraulic plant required to operate the counterweight system for the adjacent lifting bridges that provided access for boats into the former docks.

Alsop, Lyall & Störmer,
Lambeth Floating Fire Station,
London,
1991

A lightweight steel-framed and aluminium-clad structure houses a dense programme of fire service facilities: from sleeping accommodation to offices, gymnasium, lecture room and plant room. The floating building was built in North Wales, towed around the coast and up the River Thames to its permanent mooring.

However diverse our paths became, our 20-plus years working together instilled a drive to push the 'fun' of architectural expression, no matter what

Alsop & Lyall,
Splash,
Sheringham,
Norfolk, England,
1988

A public swimming baths for the small seaside town of Sheringham near Alsop's countryside home. The building was demolished in 2019 and has been replaced by The Reef Leisure Centre.

Work had gathered momentum nearer home with conservation/reuse work on the grade-1-listed Corn Exchange in Leeds (1990) that received a number of awards, as well as an all-timber public leisure pool called Splash at Sheringham on the Norfolk coast – an iconic good-value-for-money building, opened by Princess Diana in 1988. Our talented Anglo-German team grew from five to 15 relatively quickly when we moved to new office premises in Flood Street, Chelsea, in Southwest London.

Alsop, Lyall & Störmer and the Power House

Our large floor above an electricity substation saw rapid growth of the office in five years to 50 to 60 staff, and very intense work on many projects at home and abroad. Significant among these were the Cardiff Bay Visitor Centre and Barrage (1990), a new building for a computer company called Tulips in Basingstoke (1990), and rail and tube stations at Tottenham Hale (1992) and North Greenwich (1998) in London. These had some initial design input from Will, but I would end up in charge of delivering these schemes. We started a small competition-winning office in Edinburgh run by the talented Richard Murphy, which I looked after. Like other partnerships we began to concentrate more on our own projects and collaborate less, which was regrettable in the long run because it led to our parting in 1991. Will's winning scheme for the Hôtel du Département des Bouches-du-Rhône ('Le Grand Bleu', 1994) in Marseille created practice and financial pressures that as a partner I could do without, so we split. A rather sad but inevitable end to a creative relationship that had matured over 20 years. I went on to form John Lyall Architects (now Lyall Bills & Young), and to build more schemes at Cardiff Bay, Tottenham Hale Station and in Leeds.

Will designed more object-based, 'sculptural' buildings. He was always an artist at heart, which provided its own context for the work. My subsequent work was more related to the surrounding built context, using strong colour and simple forms, in projects like the Jerwood Dance House in Ipswich (2009), the Goldsmiths' Centre in London's Clerkenwell district (2011) and our London Olympics buildings (2012). But, however diverse our paths became, our 20-plus years working together instilled a drive to push the 'fun' of architectural expression, no matter what. ⌂

Alsop, Lyall & Störmer,
Tottenham Hale Station,
London,
1992

The first commission for this site incorporated a new mainline station with covered platform and café, waiting rooms and lavatories housed inside the curved aluminium tube. The design includes a 53-metre (174-foot) long painting by Bruce McLean on enamelled steel panels running the full length of the platform. Subsequent commissions for other areas of the station to connect into the underground network were carried out by John Lyall Architects.

ARCHI-TÊTES

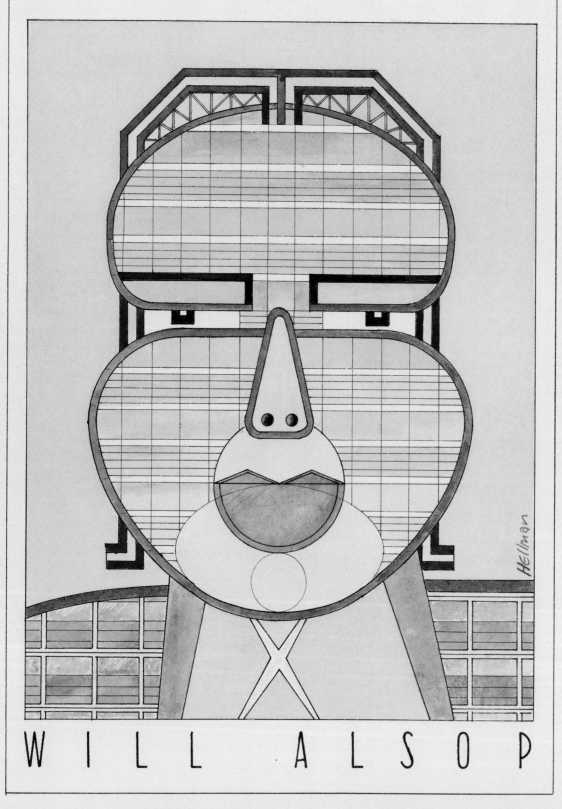

WILL ALSOP

Where There's a Will ...

Whilst lamenting the passing of so many inspirational and creative voices, **Peter Cook** can still hear the echoes of a 30-year period of iconoclasm that was the antecedent and antithesis of the circumspect introspection of architectural design today. Here he celebrates Alsop's achievements and records some shared traits. The power of Alsop's oeuvre is ever-present for those who occupy and encounter his buildings, and his persona lingers in the air for those who knew him well.

Louis Hellman,
Will Alsop 'Archi-têtes'
caricature,
Architectural Review,
November 1996

opposite: Hellman is known for his 'Archi-têtes' – caricatures of famous architects, their faces made up of bits of their buildings. He has the knack of capturing facial features with wit and a clear drawing style of his own in these cartoons.

23

Some days it gets a bit lonely. Reyner Banham and Alvin Boyarsky are now part of history, gone for over three decades but still whispering advice into my ear. Then we lost Cedric Price, Zaha Hadid and now Will Alsop. Together they gave the London architectural scene (and for that matter the global scene) a constant flow of electricity that – even in those occasional rivalrous moments – spurred one on to do bolder and clearer and better. Between them they ushered in a period of about 30 years defined by an atmosphere of creativity born out of both intelligence and, let's face it, naughtiness.

Their tangible achievements have all been well documented, yet their images are beginning to be codified: Cedric as a kind of philosophic visionary with unbelievably apposite operational strategies. He was a seer – but also a moralist and trickster – able to physically and metaphorically undo that stiff white collar when not being watched. He retained the right to cover his wall with Labour Party bunting whilst enjoying a brandy or three with the most obtuse (but amusing) right-wingers. Zaha was the screaming diva with the deft line who, behind a vociferous irritation with the sloppy and the untalented, could also be found responding like a favourite aunt to her oldest (and not necessarily famous) friends. In some ways it is the extremity of their architectural positions that invites commentators to erect around them a simplified scenario and a 'positional' definition. Will gives the same commentators a bit more difficulty. His theories and statements were never as pure as those of Cedric, his private movements never as secretive. His architectural figures were never as deft as those of Zaha, but rather multifaceted and layered – much like him.

Will the Provincial

As with Paris, Moscow and New York, London is a necessary milieu if you do not want to be pulled down by tedious conversations, do not want to hide or suffer a dearth of creative rivals. On gravitating from the Art School in Northampton to the Architectural Association (AA) School of Architecture, Will rapidly became part of the metropolitan scene. Yet a tally of his architectural and urban design projects suggest that he was far from patronising towards tough little cities – he was able to get under the skin of a town and interpret the many bits of gossip at the local bar into a witty (and always slightly provocative) take: a tube for Cardiff Bay Visitor Centre (1990); a weird pockmarked hulk for The Public in West Bromwich (2013); and chunk-cut spuds one above the other for Chips in Manchester (2009). Had his Fourth Grace for Liverpool (designed 2002–04 in preparation for Liverpool's stint as European City of Culture in 2008) been built, it would have established Will as the master of a bulbous architecture that is created out of tangible and heroically triangulated parts – ahead, by some years, of a similar direction now being attempted by many architects in China.

Alsop Architects,
Chips,
New Islington,
Manchester, England,
2009

Alsop would often name his projects after everyday items. This eight-storey housing block was described as three fat chips stacked on top of each other.

Alsop Architects,
The Fourth Grace,
Liverpool Pier Head,
England,
2002-04

The Fourth Grace or 'The Cloud' building was conceived as the centrepiece for Liverpool's bid to become the European Capital of Culture in 2008. Consisting of a 130-room boutique hotel, auditorium, museum and residential block and a sky garden with wonderful views, it was unfortunately shelved in 2004.

The interior of the Fourth Grace was to be a great example of the Alsopian use of non-orthogonal forms and interesting vignettes, to provoke a feeling of dynamism in the user.

Will the West-Londoner

Being a mobile and open observer of any place that offered an opportunity – or a good conversation – contrasted with a localness and the privacy of home life. Without ever going there, one heard Will and his wife Sheila tell of the smallness of their flat in a hidden part of Kensington, West London. The various offices were in special (or eccentric) spots: scruffy rooms at the back of the Riverside Studios in Hammersmith in the early days (I do not remember there being much of the River appearing from its tiny windows); a rather handsome Deco-ish little electricity station near the King's Road, Chelsea (The Power House). And, famously, the Battersea set-up.

Vision and practicality were merged with an eye for the quaint (not in the historical sense) in what has now become a certain kind of creative pocket between Battersea and Prince Albert Bridges on the south side of the river. A block of land inhabited by Norman Foster's office and a major outpost building for the Royal College of Art also included a tatty but characterful former tile warehouse (with a pliant landlord) that housed not only Will's architectural office, but also Squint/Opera – his son Ollie's film and communications outfit – and of course, a bar. The tour de force was Will's concept of an exhibition space – Testbed1, which opened in 2011 – with a rich mix of activities. He paid homage to my own enterprise of Art Net from the 1970s, but made it far less formal and wove it into the circuitry of the Doodle Bar (you could come and draw on the giant wall), which gained a healthy following of its own. There were Alsop-led exhibitions, performances by chamber orchestras, bands, off-the-cuff projects and carefully curated shows.

At some point the property vultures moved in and classed the site as too valuable for such a laissez-faire operation: it would have to be developed (though I do not think it actually has been). Will's office and Squint/Opera moved to trendy Bethnal Green in East London, and the Doodle Bar relocated to Bermondsey near Tower Bridge. Two years later he had passed on – which sadly seemed to echo his exile from the West.

aLL Design,
The Beach,
Battersea, London,
2013

The Beach was the riverside bar and restaurant area at the rear of the complex housing Alsop's aLL Design studio. The outdoor space was a part of the Testbed1 venue that Alsop launched as a place for design experimentation.

aLL Design,
Testbed1,
Battersea, London,
2011

The Doodle Bar and Testbed1 – designed by Alsop as part of the complex that included his aLL Design studio – became a hip place for creatives of all types to hang out, drawing on walls and contributing to a series of eclectic events and parties.

Vision and practicality were merged with an eye for the quaint (not in the historical sense) in what has now become a certain kind of creative pocket

'Turning The Tables',
Testbed1,
Battersea, London,
2011

The 'Turning the Tables' exhibition, curated
at Testbed1 by Yael Reisner in December
2011, featured 14 tables, of which
those visible here are by (left to right):
Yael Reisner with Peter Cook; Bob Sheil,
Jason Bruges; Helen & Hard; and
(in posters on the wall) Nat Chard.

Will Alsop painting in his studio in London, 2003

Alsop was a consummate artist and his artistic practice considerably overlapped with his architectural intents. Projects were instigated with painting and modelling.

The essence of certain projects can be seen in the paintings that precede them: are they sketches, are they parallel outpourings, or are they interlocutory statements revolving around the same idea?

Will the Teacher and Collaborator

With a constantly active brain and a rounded personality, Will had too much dynamic to allow him to dwell for too long on the minutiae of process – and certainly the tedium of financial caution. He was an optimist; there were possibilities in that scruffy site or grubby town, there were possibilities in that dodgy deal, and there were distinct possibilities in co-operating with a colleague or with students. The key professional partnerships were surely with John Lyall, his AA classmate, and then with Jan Störmer. He made some joint projects with architects like Mike Gold – stylistically and temperamentally quite tangential to the Alsop mode. The charm of these optimisms seemed at first to be naive, yet it was in many ways a strength and Will's natural generosity at work. As a teacher and professor, whether at the AA in London, at the Vienna University of Technology (TU Wien) or the University for the Creative Arts in Canterbury, Kent, Will burst into each studio, filled the students with enthusiasm (so sadly lacking in contemporary teaching), and – loved – left again.

Will the Avant-Gardist – the Artist

While conscious of the unfashionableness of this term, I am applying it because Will's specialness lay in his maintenance in the model of the fin-de-siècle figure: the professor-artist-raconteur-bon-vivant-enthusiast, and being essentially controversial. His paintings are certainly dynamic, special and directly painterly in comparison with almost any architect-painter – Le Corbusier's Cubism, for example, always feels too edgy and contrived. The essence of certain projects can be seen in the paintings that precede them: are they sketches, are they parallel outpourings, or are they interlocutory statements revolving around the same idea? If we had asked him this question whilst we could, we might have received a devious answer: making a building, running an office, teaching a class is great – but also a hassle. With the painting, the white surface is just there – and then you just do it!

Will the Architect

Forget the rest: Peckham Library (2000) is a skilful, considered cheer-up to dodgy old London, with its pods and its legs and its green colour and its straightforwardness. The Blizard Building (2005) makes a delightful and legitimately light-hearted incursion into South London. The Ontario College of Art & Design (OCAD) in Toronto (2004) is a tour-de-force up there in the air: 10/10 for iconography, 9/10 for making a building an art-piece. High marks for the Hôtel du Département des Bouches-du-Rhône ('Le Grand Bleu', 1994) in Marseille, an extremely mature product of a young office – beating the great and the good at the competition stage and then following through with a degree of deftness. The projects are rarely tiresome, and are brilliant (still naughty?) illustrations of what one can do with a somewhat undernourished budget and a bit of bravado. ᴆ

Will Alsop in conversation with Bob Maxwell at Art Net, London, 1970s

In late 1973, the Art Net gallery and events were established by Peter Cook with a mission to show and share ideas of architecture that were not getting commercially recognised at the time. It established itself as a sounding board for many of the global avant-garde architects. Discussing with Alsop here is Robert ('Bob') Maxwell – architect, critic and future Dean of the School of Architecture at Princeton University, New Jersey.

A SE

COURSE

ARCHIT

———

Samantha Hardingham

COND IN ECTURE

The milieu in which Alsop was educated, mixed and worked was crucial to the original architect he became. **Samantha Hardingham** describes those heady days, particularly the influence of the Architectural Association in the early 1970s and its rich menagerie of denizens of the period. She focuses on a critical and enigmatic mentor, Cedric Price, for whom Alsop worked and asserted as a profound influence on his design thinking.

Will Alsop liked to make architecture that was born out of dreams. We are not talking 'dream home' or 'fantasy architecture' but the best possible life, where people are transported – through a joyful crafting of their built environment – into the sublime. A garden of unearthly delights where people talk, argue, play, work, eat, drink, are merry, angry, beautiful, ugly, seen, hidden, together and apart. He committed his life and work as an architect to finding ways to firmly lodge the empirical into the rational, declaring 'human behaviour matters more than function'.[1] So, whilst his architectural projects have been described by critics as playful, exuberant, cartoon-like and irreverent, amongst other things, those that have been built prove to be downright practical: wide awake to the needs of their users and to the need for some *joie de vivre* for the everyday.

Schools, swimming pools, housing, libraries, a ferry terminal, train stations, office buildings, government departments, a table, a bar, a city – not to mention an opera house, prison and palace for art that did not break ground – are but a few Alsopian projects. There was no typology too big or too small to consider how to design into the 21st century, and make meaningful for future use and users. To marry these seemingly paradoxical positions is exactly what the discipline of architecture and the architectural profession demand, and as such requires a robust education in design dexterity. It relies on an innate behaviour – open-mindedness and curiosity (the dreamer), and a learned behaviour – application of the imagination to understand the rules so you can break them (the realist); and this architect landed at a time (born 1947) when he could learn from the best in this regard.

Appetiser

Alsop's combined architectural education includes periods of study at art and architecture schools as well as in practice and teaching. Each part contributed something to shaping the dreamer/imaginer but none so overtly as his time studying at the Architectural Association (AA) School of Architecture in London from 1969 to 1973 (with a year at the British School in Rome in 1972). At the AA his tutors included members of the 1960s avant-garde architectural group Archigram, David Greene and Warren Chalk, as well as Tony Dugdale and Keith Critchlow, all of whom, in different ways, equipped students with the fearless ability to experiment whilst being grounded in technical precision. It was Greene's impulse that prompted Alsop, John Lyall and a team of fellow students to submit a scheme to the international competition for Paris's Centre Pompidou (1971). Greene's interests in the consequences on architecture of a merging of information technology and nature converge with Alsop's own assertion that landscape might be granted architectural status – a movement towards a non-architecture, where architecture is given over to something or someone else.[2] The 'Paris Hills' scheme places

Dennis Crompton, Will Alsop, John Lyall,
Nora Kohen and Julius Tabacek,
Paris Hills entry for the
Centre Pompidou competition,
Paris,
1971

The competition boards show plans, sections and axonometric, a model and atmospheric colleges for the student team's entry which won them second place.

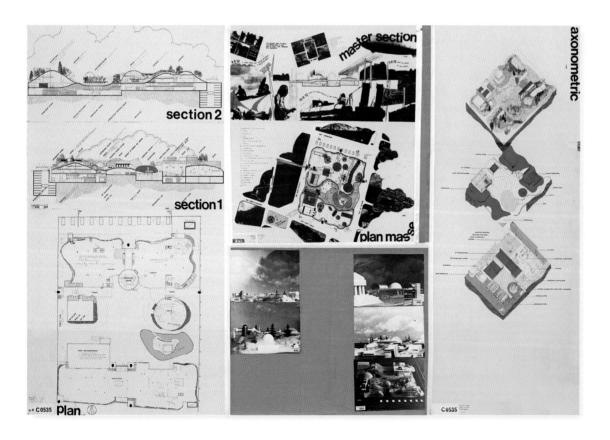

Will Alsop,
'Graffiti Manifesto',
printed in *Art Net Document Two*,
August 1974

The photo accompanied Alsop's text for
the project *Buildings and Some Frocks*. The
pneumatic structure was made by Alsop
(right) and Architectural Association Art
History tutor Harrison Dix (left). The inflatable,
made to look like a brick wall, is covered in
slogans about current issues facing the city.

THE DESIGN POLEMIC-CUM-PARABLE ON THE IMPACT OF COMMUNITY ACTION ON DESIGN ECHOES HIS BOSS'S METHOD AND MODE

much of the art centre beneath rolling hills with some low building event objects and trees punctuating the landscape.

Other Archigram members, Dennis Crompton (who is also named in the Pompidou scheme as having added his professional qualification to the team entry) and Peter Cook, were also teaching at the AA and ever-present on the local (becoming ever more international) architectural scene. Cook had spent two years as the Director of the Institute of Contemporary Arts (ICA) and, disillusioned with its activities, went on to set up Art Net in 1973 – a non-profit organisation offering a rival programme of art and architecture events. There was a venue in West Central Street, Covent Garden. The idea had been born out of a conversation with Cedric Price and funded by politician and art collector Alistair McAlpine.

Alsop presented what could be understood as his first architectural manifesto entitled *Buildings and Some Frocks,* as part of an exhibition at Art Net called 'Five Young Architects', held from 14 September to 2 October 1974.

Alfons Oberhofer, Mark Fisher, Mark Primack and Paul Shepheard featured alongside Alsop. A video recording sadly cuts out just before Alsop presents his work to a packed room including critics Cedric Price, James Gowan, Dalibor Vesely, Ingrid Morris and Alvin Boyarsky.[3] We see Alsop in the audience, seated on one of the deckchairs, with several panels behind him on the wall. Rather strangely, the camera suddenly zooms in on him, he glances directly into the lens – as if to give a cue – and then all goes dark. Thankfully, Cook produced a printed magazine, *Art Net Document Two* (August 1974), which includes a reprint of Alsop's presentation for a series of drawings for 13 buildings. It is evident that he has been working in Price's office for about a year by then – the design polemic-cum-parable on the impact of community action on design echoes his boss's method and mode, not least the paper, format and typescript of the text pieces themselves, which closely resemble the communications produced by the Cedric Price Architects (CPA) office.

Entrée

And so to the second course – or perhaps given both Price and Alsop's fondness for a good lunch, the main course: five years part-time as an architectural assistant at CPA, in Bloomsbury, London (1973–7), working the rest of the week as sculpture tutor at Saint Martin's School of Art (now Central Saint Martins) in London.[4] The three foundational projects – Fun Palace (1961), Potteries Thinkbelt (1964) and the New Aviary at London Zoo (1965) – were but decade-old news for Price. Each project had helped to consolidate a reputation and a theory of architecture centred on a principled pursuit of the dynamics of time, which put learning, people and participation at the centre of every project, supported by a technical interest in making the most with the least. The office job list at the time included the government-funded *Air Structures: A Survey* (1971),[5] researched and written with engineer Frank Newby, which in turn listed other CPA projects: Phun City (1970–71) – pneumatic enclosures for a music festival in Sussex; Southend (1971) – a pneumatic pillow roof stretching the full length of a high street in Essex that lifted and settled according to temperature and precipitation; McAppy (1976) – a design strategy for improving building site conditions; and River Clyde (1973) – an ideas competition for the rethinking of Glasgow in Scotland following the demise of the shipbuilding industry. The design proposal invited a participatory process for engaging all residents and people passing through to develop the new plans for the city.

Cedric Price,
River Clyde ideas competition,
Scotland,
1973

right: An aerial view of the site with sketch proposal, looking west. The project sought to make new use of Glasgow's river as a socio-industrial testbed to include food farms (for study and supply), a floating jungle (for fun), new transport methods and new forms of industrial experimentation such as manufacturing of prefabricated floating housing (making use of existing skills and cultural heritage). It calls to mind Alsop's own collages for urban plans, or what he preferred to call 'big architecture': Barcelona (2003), Barnsley (2003), Bradford and Middlehaven (2004).

Will Alsop,
SuperCity,
2005

left: Pages from the accompanying catalogue, published by Urbis (Manchester), for an exhibition of Alsop's project for a city stretching from Liverpool to Hull along the M62 motorway that coincided with the then Labour government's plans for sustainable communities. Carrying echoes of the River Clyde competition, Alsop's polemical project resonates with some of Price's work that looks for practical solutions born out of political provocation.

Letter from Will Alsop of
Cedric Price Architects
to Professor Joanne Robden
of the Royal College of Art,
21 November 1974

opposite: The letter concerns design research around making improvements to on-site protective clothing in conjunction with Price's McAppy project.

Professor Joanne Robden
Fashion Department
RCA
Kensington Gore
LONDON SW7   21 November 1974

Dear Professor Robden,

We are currently engaged as consultants to a firm of building contractors
in order to investigate methods of improving site conditions. One of the
areas under investigation is protective clothing.

Would anyone in your Department be interested in doing research into this
subject? I enclose a brief outline of relevant background material for
your information. If there is an interest perhaps we could arrange a
meeting in the near future in order to discuss the matter further.

Yours truly,

Will Alsop
(Cedric Price)

Cedric Price Architects,
Inter-Action Centre,
London,
1981

below: Will Alsop stands at the northwest corner of the Kentish Town site in 1974. He and office colleague Paul Hyett shared the task of making site visits and oversaw completion of the first phase: the concrete slab and footings with drainage and the two-storey steel main frame and roof trusses.

bottom: Following completion of the first phase, there was a pause in construction for almost two years whilst further funds were raised, and during this time the frame was occupied by a temporary funfair, amongst other activities.

The young architect witnessed first-hand how to put theories of construction and community action into practice as assistant on Inter-Action, Kentish Town, London, a project that spanned the years 1970–81. The building had been commissioned by the Inter-Action Trust, a charity set up by US-born Ed Berman based on principles of community self-help with a focus on promoting local arts events, festivals, media facilities, a city farm and the first community architecture service in Europe, amongst other things. In the US the role of the architect was generally understood to be at the service of the community; by contrast, in the UK the role was still considered very much an elite profession that might design public architecture but was unlikely to engage with the public. Price used Inter-Action to turn all this on its head. In response to a vote by 3,500 local residents for a new arts resource centre, he designed a purpose-built 'mechanism' for several different interest groups to occupy simultaneously as well as facilitate the changing of minds as required. Where the Fun Palace had been conceived as a 'Giant Space Mobile' requiring a skilled technical workforce to run things day-to-day, Inter-Action was the pocket version capable of being adapted by its users.

Cedric Price Architects,
'Office: Reason, Operation, Objective' –
confidential internal office memo,
27 July 1973

The single A4 page, handwritten by Price, sets out the operational 'rules'
for the office and in particular what he expected of his employees.

The architectural principles for the two projects were very similar: a main frame designed to receive various enclosures and services that in turn could be rearranged as and when required. The building handover was accompanied by a construction/deconstruction manual, which itself had a use-by date of 20 years hence to ensure that the building remained relevant to the organisation. Price understood that social, political, cultural and environmental conditions are constantly changing, and his architecture would be designed with those dynamics in mind. Alsop remembered it to be the most exciting time; a funfair one week, a football match the next, the mere outline of a building offered no end of possibilities for free-spirited occupancy and community stewardship.

Something for Afters

On Alsop's arrival at the CPA offices in Alfred Place in summer of 1973 – from where the practice operated for 40 years – a confidential memo was circulated to all staff, setting out the operational rules for the office and in particular what Price expected of his employees. It was entitled 'Office: Reason, Operation, Objective', and starts with three quotes: 'Nagging is the necessary repetition on the wilfully inattentive'; 'To ask the same questions twice may mean the question is nonsense'; 'To produce the same answer twice is to assume the role of the machine.'

Alsop's own offices operated in different times and often along very different lines, but he engaged firmly and cordially with his clients and developed experimental consultation practices with often large communities and sometimes whole cities. His fascination with people and generous sharing of knowledge, hard work and fun are a debt to Price. The memo's concluding sentence resounds: 'Always remember you might not know who (and under what condition) can make the best of what you have just done!' ᴁ

Notes
1. Kenneth Powell, *Will Alsop Book 1*, Lawrence King (London), 2001, p 25.
2. *Ibid*, p 30.
3. 'Critics Choice – Five Young Architects 1 & 2': https://www.youtube.com/watch?v=BRtpMIFlIJk.
4. Ian Chilvers (ed), *The Oxford Dictionary of Art*, Oxford University Press (Oxford), 2004: www.oxfordreference.com/view/10.1093/oi/authority.201108 03100533679?rskey=jb33eu&result=1.
5. Cedric Price, Frank Newby and Robert H Suan, *Air Structures: A Survey*, HM Stationery Office (London), 1971.

'ALWAYS REMEMBER YOU MIGHT NOT KNOW WHO (AND UNDER WHAT CONDITION) CAN MAKE THE BEST OF WHAT YOU HAVE JUST DONE!'

Nigel Coates

WILLIE WONKY ARTY-TECTURE

AND THE FACTORY

Will Alsop,
Painting workshop with visiting
students from the Vienna
University of Technology (TU
Wien),
Chongqing,
China,
c 2015

A typical painting workshop where students work on one large drawing collectively. Will's anarchic ways were welcomed by the students and complemented the more formal teaching ethos adopted across the majority of schools of architecture.

Nigel Coates lets us into the creative world of messy play that Alsop favoured as a way to teach architecture – the live-in, eat-in, drink-in workshop. Such practices disrupted assumed modes of operation for architects and provoked new spatial and formal opportunities. His workshops, studios and lectures were a challenging mixture of kindergarten, party and questioning observations, all conducted with critical and colourful exuberance.

You're fresh out of architecture school, and embarking on a career in architecture. A bit of teaching could earn some much-needed pennies. Later, when you've got plenty of work, time with students might give you a rest from the office. For many of my peers, tutoring has been nourishment for the soul, but teach too much and you risk fulfilling George Bernard Shaw's maxim, 'Those that can, do; those that can't, teach.' Will Alsop had a foot in both camps, practice and pedagogy, and was all the happier for it. His methods were rooted in a loose-fit, visceral, lived experience that emancipated all who dared get involved.

A Live-In Experiment

There's a video on YouTube about a teaching retreat of Will's at Las Heras in Spain.[1] In 2016, a troupe of seven students turned up at the rural country house where participants would be staying during the week-long workshop. They included two students from the newly formed London School of Architecture (LSA) who were being mentored by Will's office. In a back-to-basics group exercise, the aim was to wean everyone off the big house in favour of a place that would generate 'houseness' from scratch. In the video we see participants fired up with bonhomie heading for the woods. The result may not look that effective as protection from the elements, but it was the event that mattered. This kind of lived experience was characteristically Will's, and typical of his approach to teaching.

Will Alsop,
Las Heras workshop,
Spain,
2016

A summer camp with seven architecture students. They lived an experiment that included not only a physical output – a timber shelter in the woods for stargazing – but also lots of collective eating and drinking.

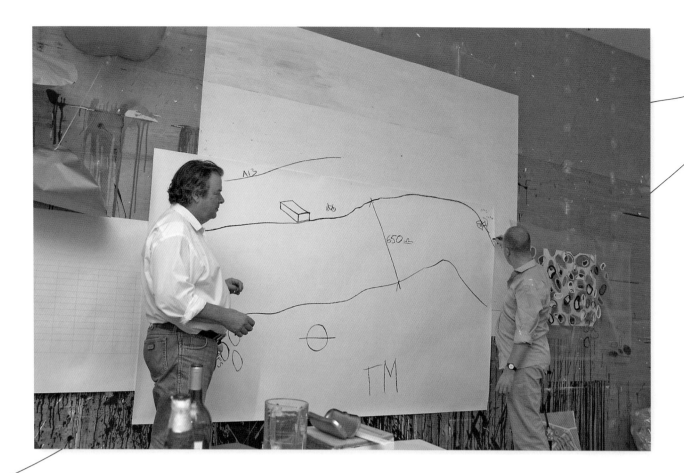

Will Alsop in the studio with
architect Ian Abley working
on ideas about megastructures,
Battersea, London,
c 2006

In an effort to overturn any vestige of architectural
OCD, the creative studio would be equipped with
materials for meetings that engaged visitors directly
with drawing out ideas. Whether working with client
groups or students, Will enjoyed the togetherness of
collective creativity.

Apparently Will liked nothing more than a closed-circuit Big Brother. Las Heras was like a cross between the Architectural Association (AA) rural campus at Hooke Park, Dorset, and the Burning Man annual festival in the Arizona desert. The detachment from the usual academic environment would help set aside the usual tropes. Whether students were building full-sized prototypes, painting or model-making, he wanted them to feel disconcerted, challenged and to gain insights that stemmed from an inner force. He tapped into a thread in creative education that stems from the British art-school tradition of learning through doing – a tradition that, despite huge rewards, is more under threat than ever from the streamlining of education as business.

He wasn't really head-of-school material; rather the superhero who'd make an occasional appearance to disrupt proceedings. Gradually the students would be drawn into a brotherhood. They would start a session by pouring a round of drinks, roll up their sleeves and tackle some abstract question he was toying with at the time, a cathartic éclat that short-circuited the usual gambits.

Such a proposition – something offbeat or dysfunctional – was intended to blow their preconceptions apart. You would be invited to attack that choice, devastate it, and then sift through the rubble in search of ideas that could survive the detritus. It was like war without the bombs, and a pitch for overthrowing the inherent oppression in the well-rehearsed methods of architectural design. Solutions needed to emerge from the gut, and not by rehashing design memes gleaned from social media. It was as though the freedom of sketching would be enlarged into a collective activity where there was no place to hide.

It was as though the freedom of sketching would be enlarged into a collective activity where there was no place to hide

Painting was always Will's creative medium of choice. With vast canvases and buckets of paint, he sought out expressionist immediacy, and not the ponderous intimacy of the sketchbook page. Like Zaha Hadid's drawing (another AA graduate), but unlike the precision in hers, his painting would be the alchemical means of freeing the spirit. Will's painting style was oversized, colourful and gestural. He made images free from gravity, allowing him to switch scales and inject life into inert matter. The blobs and boxes grew spindly legs and, like cartoon zoomorphs, wobbled around looking for somewhere to shelter for the night.

His creative bouts would stem from a mix of shock tactics and collective Will-power.

As with students, the studio workshop would extend to carefully chosen others, and would nurture audacity. Everything and anything was allowed – everyday objects, parts of the body or cartoon-like transformations of the same. Like group therapy, the workshop put these specimens through a kind of mincer that detached them from their origins and prepared them as candidates for buildings.

Painting/model experiment,
Battersea, London,
c 2010

Will engaged in a continuous process of experimentation and engaged his team in all phases of the process – from graphics to painting to model-making and bookmaking. At work here is Mark Boyce, a graphic designer and member of the Painting Studio at Alsop's office.

Alsop Architects,
Sharp Centre for Design,
Ontario College of Art & Design (OCAD),
Toronto, Canada,
2004

All Alsop's iconic buildings began on canvas then
translated to sketch. The Sharp Centre was one of several
boxes elevated on wobbly stilts. Its conception was as
much an attractive shape as it was the idea of a building.

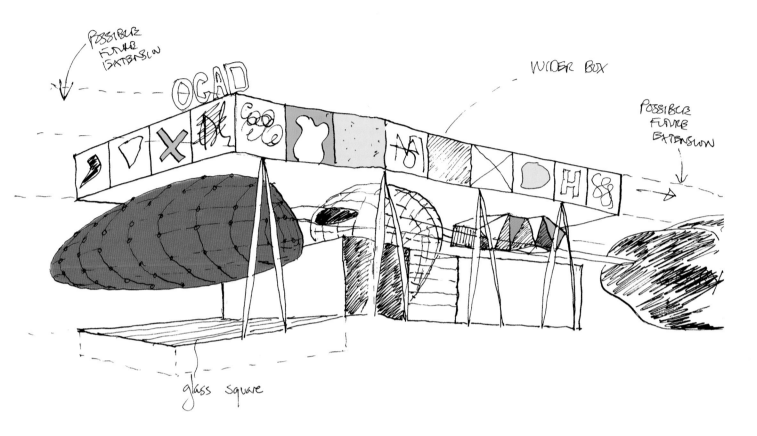

Sidestepping the baseline seriousness of the architect was paramount for Will: play would speak to his inner voice as much as it did to his artist peers

Playing the Field

Play was certainly part of the ethos, and had been since the
early days. When Will was a student at the AA in the 1960s and
early 70s, it was a period heavily influenced by counterculture
magazine *OZ* and its founder Richard Neville's book *Playpower*
(1970).[2] Sidestepping the baseline seriousness of the architect was
paramount for Will: play would speak to his inner voice as much
as it did to his artist peers.

I first came across Will when he was a tutor at London's Saint
Martin's School of Art. He was one of a group called The Locker
Room that taught my first boyfriend António Lagarto on the
so-called Sculpture A course, a concept-driven experiment in
educational deprivation. During one six-week project, students
were forbidden to talk and would have to arrive at college early
enough to wear one of a limited number of belts. Like monks,
they were told to work in silence and were encouraged to 'play
solo' to eschew any stock solution. At the conclusion of the
project, Will warmed to António's work – not a sculpture as such,
but a horror story in the form of a text. It must have primed Will's
commitment to push against this conceptual austerity.

Will believed that if you start with the ugly, the result might very well be beautiful

In the late 1990s, Will was elected professor at the Technische Universität Wien, and so made trips to Vienna once a month. He was always thirsty for new experiences and loved travelling. Airports were incubators of freedom, and the elastic time zones gave him the chance to work on his own thoughts. These visits afforded him engagement with a formal academic environment he could legitimately contest. Herr Professor was permitted to be Herr Disruptor. He would throw students in at the deep end. They loved working with him. And in a perverse way, he thrived on the inherent formality at the university. It gave him the kind of rigid containment he could push against.

Moving the Goalposts

Will's approach was very close to mine at the Royal College of Art (RCA), where I was head of the Department of Architecture (1995–2011) and why, in 2003, I invited him to be a Visiting Professor at our school. I'd modelled the architecture department on art-school principles of thinking-and-doing, and he was a natural fit. As a resident of West London he was keen to join us; 'Of course I'll do it. The RCA is my local architecture school.' He would occasionally stage a seminar for the students. One such event was an in-camera seminar on the subject of 'ugliness', which was quite a difficult starting point for most RCA students who have a way of making even the ugliest output look pretty. He knew exactly what he was doing. As his long-term team member Christophe Egret recalls, Will believed that if you start with the ugly, the result might very well be beautiful.

Before Will's professorship began, he and I invented a new prize for graduates: the Will Alsop Prize for Urbanism. It was a means to encourage students to work at a bigger scale. At the Degree Show 2000, graduate George Wade was its first recipient. By that time, Will had the burgeoning office he'd always wanted, but that brought problems of its own, namely greater emphasis on production rather than the much more invigorating processes of conception. George, along with former student of the Slade School of Fine Art, Tim Thornton and graphic designer Mark Boyce, were invited to power the newly formed Painting Studio which Will embedded inside the main architectural office.

In all his teaching endeavours, he wanted to share some of the freedom he experienced by painting – and in opposition to what, to him, was a stuffy and worthy profession. Any student of his must have been affected by his courage and creative freedom. Even the most timid of operators will have learned to think bigger, brighter and more courageously. ᴆ

Notes
1. Savage Mills, 'Las Heras, Will Alsop's Educational Retreat', 2017: www.youtube.com/watch?v=g0oWuNatpDQ.
2. Richard Neville, *Playpower: Exploring the International Underground*, Jonathan Cape (London), 1970.

Will Alsop painting in his studio
at the office in Battersea,
London,
c 2010

Painting was as integral to Will's office as any model-building workshop might be in others. It focused the alchemical process of creation by short-circuiting the architect's inherent rationalism.

Paul Finch

aLL Design,
Neuron Pod, London
School of Medicine
and Dentistry,
Queen Mary University,
Whitechapel, London,
2019

An addition to the Blizard
Building campus, a building
in the shape of a neuron
cell. Once again Alsop defies
the assumption that form
following function will result
in standardised (and probably
boring) outcomes.

One of Alsop & Lyall's first built works was a swimming pool at Sheringham in Norfolk, close to Alsop's family home, and was a long, extruded form. Paul Finch followed Alsop's entire career through the eyes of a journalist, making the connection between the use of the formal extrusion as design tactic and many of the buildings and schemes that came later. Coupled with Alsop's non-belief in the old 'form follows function' idiom, this allowed him to create vivacious architectural designs, urban districts and whole cities.

Will Alsop and Paul Finch,
London,
1995

On the occasion of Will Alsop presenting some recent projects and in conversation with Paul Finch, editor of the *Architects' Journal* at the time, at Crowbar Coffee in London.

Will Alsop was a generator of architectural and planning ideas at city and regional scale. But he also relished the opportunity to design and deliver specific buildings, seeing little distinction between a propositional idea for, say, a huge swathe of countryside, and the detailed design and planning of an individual element within it. In recent UK architectural history, only Richard Rogers operated in anything like the same way; and while their buildings are very different, there are certain similarities of approach – the use of vivid colour, the expressed structure, the dramatic intervention producing an entirely new and memorable context rather than merely 'fitting in'.

Curiously enough, Alsop and team, including his fellow Architectural Association (AA) student John Lyall, were placed second in the competition for the Centre Pompidou in Paris, which Rogers and Renzo Piano won in 1971. In that exciting and unpredictable period, where the avant-garde seemed to be based in and around the AA in Bedford Square and the world of Peter Cook, Art Net and Archigram in Covent Garden, Alsop and Lyall both worked for the insider/outsider Cedric Price, completing their architectural education in his offices in nearby Alfred Place.

Alsop & Lyall,
Riverside Studios
redevelopment,
London,
1982

Flirting with Postmodernism: Alsop & Lyall's proposal for a riverside site in Hammersmith, West London, emerged after the location of their office in Riverside Studios.

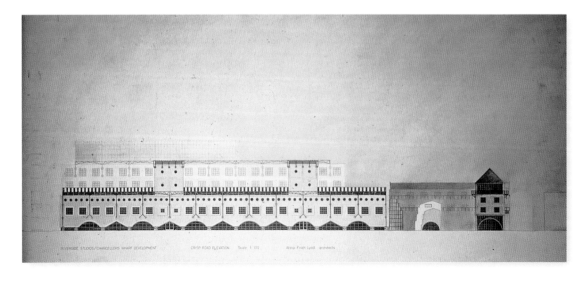

But they were their own architects and in 1981 established an office in Riverside Studios, Hammersmith, boldly proposing a very postmodern (unbuilt) replacement. Their first building was the Splash swimming pool complex in Sheringham, Norfolk (1988), an exercise in glulam timber construction which was quite shocking for the conservationist-minded locals, but nevertheless a popular success.

The inevitable horizontality of a swimming pool complex set a precedent for much that was to follow. The spectacular Cardiff Bay Visitor Centre (1990), won in competition, was a sensational visual intervention for the Welsh capital's harbour area and remained in place for many years after the closure date originally planned. Will once told me in conversation that he had always wanted to design a building with the same shape as his oval-tube cigarette lighter – he seized the opportunity.

Any impracticalities generated by the unusual shape (for example the use of sheep-pen rails to stop children falling into the gap between the floor and the curved façade) were outweighed by the impact of the structure on its environment, whatever the season, time of day or weather condition. Will had little time for 'form-follows-function' zealotry, even arguing that 'form has nothing to do with function'. I adapted his remark to describe what he was getting at: 'form swallows function'. By which I meant that

in his world, the function of a building was not limited to the activities contained within the building envelope, but to its effect or contribution to street, neighbourhood, quarter or city. The functionalist tradition did not seem to involve much fun.

Colour, Form and Mass

It was never necessarily true that all Will's work had to involve vibrant, painterly colouring. For example, the Hamburg Ferry Terminal (1993) looked at the time, and still looks like, an exercise in structural efficiency, another piece of horizontal architecture echoing the container ships increasingly evident in the city's huge docks complex. It was designed with Jan Störmer, who had become a named partner in the practice in 1990.

Alsop & Störmer,
Hôtel du Département des Bouches-du-Rhône
('Le Grand Bleu'),
Marseille, France,
1994

View of the completed building with the teardrop-shaped block of the 'Délibératif' (the council debating chamber open to the public) in the foreground and central block on three-storey-high X-shaped columns. 'Le Grand Bleu' marked the emergence of the practice as a major international presence, following a hard-fought international competition.

However, when the chance came to deploy colour in addition to form and mass, he delivered in spades. Nowhere more so than in what is probably his best building, won in competition with John Lyall: 'Le Grand Bleu' (1994) – or, to give it its formal name, the Hôtel du Département des Bouches-du-Rhône, Marseille – is a triumph. It was the first time a younger British architect had won an overseas competition against Norman Foster, supplementing the Hamburg building with a piece of public architecture (an administrative headquarters for the region) which was as imposing as it was imaginative. It incorporated a slightly curved ground floor, which Will included to make it difficult for the substantial entrance lobby to be turned into a commercial exhibition centre. The building, an assembly of curved and orthogonal linked blocks, still has both gravity and grandeur, as well as a sense of delight generated by the Mediterranean blue façade.

Although these two continental buildings secured his reputation within the architectural community, it was several years before Will came to prominence in the eyes of the UK public. When it happened it was in spectacular fashion with the Peckham Library building (2000) which won the RIBA Stirling Prize in the same year. The awards event was televised for the first time; in combination with the remarkable and memorable form of the library structure and the shock of a cultural building making a

mark in a poor South London area (best known for a TV series about Peckham's street-trader demi-monde), this was headline stuff.

From an architectural point of view, the library was a radical departure from received wisdom about the appropriate way to plan this building type – that is to say, creating a route at ground level, taking visitors from the entrance to a central space with no level change. At Peckham, you arrive at a building where the front half of the lower floors has been cut away, creating an elevated 'box on stilts'. Then having entered, you are forced to take a lift to reach the library space. This was heresy for some architects, but there was a prosaic functional explanation for the plan. First, the building was more than a library; it also offered social service and housing advice, so library-only design conventions were not the only consideration. More important was the possibility of lifting the spirits, metaphorically and almost literally, of library users by providing them with facilities at height – offering long, dramatic views towards central London.

Structurally daring (the young engineer was Hanif Kara), visually spectacular, again exploiting vivid colour, this was a worthy Stirling Prize winner, fulfilling a social as well as an architectural programme by raising the profile of the area, and which has grown in popularity ever since. It provided a precedent for another design for a horizontal block supported by pilotis – a more extreme

Alsop & Störmer,
Peckham Library,
London,
2000

A view at night from across the plaza shows the offices and administration in the vertical element with the main library in the overhanging block and red 'shading' tongue poking out over the roof. The library transformed the image of a downtrodden inner suburb with a building which won the Stirling Prize for its vitality, innovation and daring.

Alsop Architects, Sharp Centre for Design,
Ontario College of Art & Design (OCAD),
Toronto, Canada,
2004

An extreme version of Peckham Library, a bravura, typology-defying exercise that looks just as good in real life as it did in the early visualisations.

version of Peckham inasmuch as virtually all the building is contained in the elevated horizontal box. The Sharp Centre for Design at the Ontario College of Art & Design (OCAD) in Toronto, Canada (2004) is one of those rare buildings which looks exactly like its visualisations – an extraordinary built diagram, where the decoration comprises windows and cladding elements which make the building resemble an exotic piece of nougat.

Will continued to work in Toronto for the rest of his life, and late buildings included two metro stations completed in 2017, which are light years away from the usual downbeat nature of that building type. He had cut his teeth in transport architecture in London, with the Tottenham Hale Station (1992) and then North Greenwich underground station, completed as part of the Jubilee Line Extension in 1998, shortlisted for the Stirling Prize a year later. The impressive design is about volume rather than area, featuring dramatically angled blue tile-clad columns. It provided inspiration for a much more significant design for the Crossrail station at Paddington (commissioned in 1992), which like many good designs was abandoned as that programme suffered from endless delays and procurement regime change.

Other designs for London fared better, for example the Blizard Building in Whitechapel for the London School of Medicine and Dentistry, Queen Mary University (2005), an education/research project that managed to bring colour and drama to a prosaic building brief. In a quite different context, so too did the Palestra office building on Blackfriars Road (2006), where a speculative development brief was transformed by architectural imagination into an office building with real brio – a large space (37,400 square metres (403,000 square feet)) but not a tower, sitting comfortably in its urban situation. It has familiar Alsop elements: a raised box, stacked horizontal volumes, curvature and lively colours. The office space works in both open-plan and cellular arrangements, so functionally efficient, but for Will the essential element was the contribution the architecture could make as a visual urban addition in a neighbourhood that included Tate Modern. There is a specific artwork on the street elevation opposite Southwark Jubilee Line underground station: geometrical patterning bonded onto the glass panels, albeit less flamboyant than the original concept sketches.

Alsop Architects,
Blizard Building,
London School of Medicine and Dentistry,
Queen Mary University,
Whitechapel, London,
2005

An illustration of Alsop's maxim that 'form has nothing to do with function', providing a science-based institution with buildings and interiors that please both the eye and the mind.

SMC Alsop,
Palestra,
London,
2006

A rare excursion into the world of speculative office design generated this striking landmark on Blackfriars Road which transformed the area around Southwark Jubilee Line underground station. The building acts as a marker for a route to the nearby Tate Modern art gallery.

Alsop Architects,
Calypso,
Rotterdam,
The Netherlands,
2013

The 20-storey tower is a built reminder of the controversial Rotterdam Centraal urban masterplan Alsop produced for the city in 2001.

Programme Vacuum

In retrospect, this is an architect who worked best when responding to a specific and demanding brief, to which he could bring a creative interpretation that might turn the formal programme on its head. Less successful were those instances where he not only operated as the architect, but became involved in defining the programme for the building – which he might well have already conceived. Two examples make the point: one unbuilt, the other delivered but in unhappy circumstances.

In Liverpool, Will won a competition to design an addition to the waterfront, referred to by locals as the 'Fourth Grace', in 2004. His spectacular proposal, called 'The Cloud', would have transformed the area and, depending on your point of view, either dragged the city into the 21st century or wrecked views of the internationally famous waterfront. The truth is that the client, led by the city council, never really knew what it wanted, and the designers filled the programme vacuum by adding multiple elements that eventually frightened off the client, nervous of a repeat of the Millennium Dome overspend (even though that building came in under budget and on time). The architect retired hurt – and out of pocket.

In West Bromwich, The Public (2008), another Alsopian horizontal box, was built with the help of substantial National Lottery / Arts Council funding, but closed in 2013 after only five years of operation. The building attracted nearly one million people during its life as an arts and creative centre, but the lack of a committed client with the expertise and funding to manage such an ambitious project proved fatal. The precedent project was the Cedric Price / Joan Littlewood 'Fun Palace' from 1960, where it was envisaged that anything and everything could happen all the time. It was a self-created brief in the absence of a real client and unsurprisingly was never built, though the ideas were influential. Will's misfortune in West Bromwich was to have a client never really equipped to live up to his ideas.

Modification via Nature

Despite the various incarnations of the Alsop office, largely stemming from his self-admitted weakness in financial management, the built output never ceased. Although not invited to produce anything for the London Olympics of 2012, international commissions continued to flow. An unusual project in Singapore, the regeneration of Clarke Quay (2006) – his first major Asian work – showed another side of Alsop's design interests: modification of the built environment via nature. In this instance, shading and cooling is provided without the use of air-conditioning, winning the project a variety of awards. It was a take on an earlier project: the shortlisted competition design for the British Pavilion at the 1992 Seville Expo which shows an opening roof that allowed a helium-filled mini-Zeppelin to rise above the building, providing shade during the hottest hours of the day and producing a visual spectacle.

Amidst many studies and never-to-be projects, other Asian work did come to fruition, notably the Gao Yang international cruise terminal in Shanghai (2010), heralding in the final incarnation of his practice, aLL Design, established with Marcus Rosello in 2011. Spectacular sculptural pieces like the Neuron Pod (2019), next to the Blizard Building, were undertaken at the same time as residential tower proposals, which could be based on Will's 'knock nothing down' mantra as to how one might combine old and new (see the article by Marcos Rosello in this issue, pp 110–17).

Will Alsop had an incessant urge to design buildings that could be delivered, and his output – despite the financial rollercoaster of his practice life – was immense. He was a one-off in the pantheon of great architects from the past 50 years, gregarious, hospitable and inspirational. He, and his approach to architecture, are much missed. ⌀

aLL Design,
The Public,
West Bromwich,
West Midlands, England,
2013

Study model for The Public arts centre. The sectional arrangement shows large independent volumes for different activities floating inside the main box.

Neil Thomas

YES, THIS ARCHITE

IS
CTURE

aLL Design,
Three Towers development
at Capital Interchange Way,
Brentford, London,
2014–17

Visualisation from ground level looking
towards the middle tower.

Structural engineer **Neil Thomas** describes some of the memorable encounters and collaborations with Alsop, particularly the Cardiff Bay Visitor Centre that Alsop maintained was inspired by his disposable cigarette lighter. A creative relationship maintained over a timeline that spanned nearly 30 years, Thomas conveys their way of working together that was fuelled by a deep desire to dare to dream met with breathtaking and credible design solutions.

There are two architects whom I have had the great pleasure of working with, and both have made a huge impact on the wider design world: Will Alsop and another fellow alumnus of London's Architectural Association (AA) School of Architecture, Mark Fisher.[1] They shared an intense interest in designing temporary structures and buildings, and challenged the way we, Atelier One, have worked as structural engineers. Although pursuing very different careers, their work collectively exudes a shared delight in the world and delighting people in the world. As I wrote in *Liquid Threshold: Atelier One*, published in 2009 to celebrate our office's 20th anniversary: 'The influence of Will Alsop on architecture is felt everywhere.'[2]

I was introduced to Will for the first time in 1988 by engineer Anthony (Tony) Hunt at his home in Cirencester, a pretty market town in Gloucestershire. I was a director at Anthony Hunt Associates in their London office (1988–9). Where

Alsop, Lyall & Störmer,
Cardiff Bay Visitor
Centre,
Wales,
1990

Once the exhibition that was housed inside was over, the building could be repurposed for another unknown use elsewhere, so a series of prefabricated elliptical slices were developed based upon transport widths.

Tony was one of the most generous people I have ever met, Will was the most mesmerising – we talked a lot about architecture, art and, significantly, temporary buildings.

Travel forward to 1990 and Will phoned to see if Atelier One would be interested in working on a design for a new visitor centre in the Welsh capital, Cardiff. At that time his studio was at The Power House in Chelsea, an area of London better known for fashion than architecture. We were in Soho and it was not so easy to get from one to the other, but because we had another client, fashion designers Stephen Marks and Nicole Farhi, not 100 metres (300 feet) away, it gave me a good excuse to spend more time at Will's office. Alsop & Lyall's studio was magical with all sorts of intriguing things lying about everywhere – art, big models and a really creative bunch of people. What also stood out was Will's unabashed use of colour, which brought another level of joy to his buildings.

Everything But Smoke and Mirrors

Cardiff Bay Visitor Centre (1990) was a building designed to house a temporary exhibition for the proposed new Cardiff Bay Barrage. At our first meeting for the project, Will did something very unexpected – he held up a cigarette lighter (the classic disposable plastic kind made by Bic – nothing glamorous) and said, 'That is what I want.'

What developed was a building which signifies change. It was intended that it be demountable with a life span of five years. The 50-metre (160-foot) long building was made up from 2.4-metre (8-foot) wide by 14-metre (46-foot) sections so that each could be lifted individually onto a 12-metre (40-foot) trailer ready to be transported to site from the manufacturers in Notting Hill. To reduce costly groundworks and ground interfaces, it was lifted off the ground on short, angled legs – more than footings, not quite pilotis. A composite structure was formed by combining a ply skin to a light steel frame with a layer of insulation and PVC membrane over the top to provide waterproofing. In typical Will fashion, he then added the series of squiggly cut-outs in the plywood which, due to the translucency of the membrane and insulation, produce spots of natural light throughout the enclosure.

The building became very popular with the people of Cardiff – a notable piece of modern architecture for the city. After its extended but temporary life, the client – the Cardiff Bay Development Corporation – decided to keep it but to move it along the bay to feature as part of a new development. Instead of breaking it into slices to transport it, Mammoet (the heavy structure moving specialists) lifted the whole building onto a multi-tracked vehicle and drove it down the bay to its new home. It remained there until 2010 – far beyond its sell-by date – then was dismantled and put into storage.

A view from inside the Visitor Centre shows the light steel frame, plywood cladding and white PVC membrane on the exterior. The cuts in the plywood sheet admit natural light through the membrane, animating the space.

A night-time view of the completed structure with the exhibition installation inside and Cardiff Bay in the background. Columns meet almost cross-legged underneath the main enclosure, giving the appearance at night of a large volume floating above the ground.

Following the Cardiff Bay Visitor
Centre, Atelier One worked on a
whole series of buildings with Will
and his office which were nothing less
than groundbreaking. Notably, we
collaborated on the competition for the
Hôtel du Département des Bouches-
du-Rhône in Marseille in 1994 that
became the winning scheme 'Le Grand
Bleu'. In winning, Will Alsop achieved
the status he deserved. As Atelier One
was only a small structural engineering

practice at the time, our involvement
was commensurate with our size.
Arup were the main engineers on the
project, but most excitingly for us, we
were introduced to the truly creative
engineers Chris McCarthy and Guy
Battle, who built on Will's radical
approach to building form, even
incorporating a version of the Cardiff
Bay Visitor Centre on the roof.

One of Will's most radical designs
was his entry for the British Pavilion
for the Seville Expo in 1992. Two
large doors in the roof would open
to reveal a huge inflatable that would
rise out to sit above the building.
The building was fun and eccentric.
It broke with convention, and was a
beautiful essay on Will's ideas and
ambition. Although close to winning
the competition, it was perhaps a little
too radical – something he was all too
familiar with hearing but that never
discouraged him.

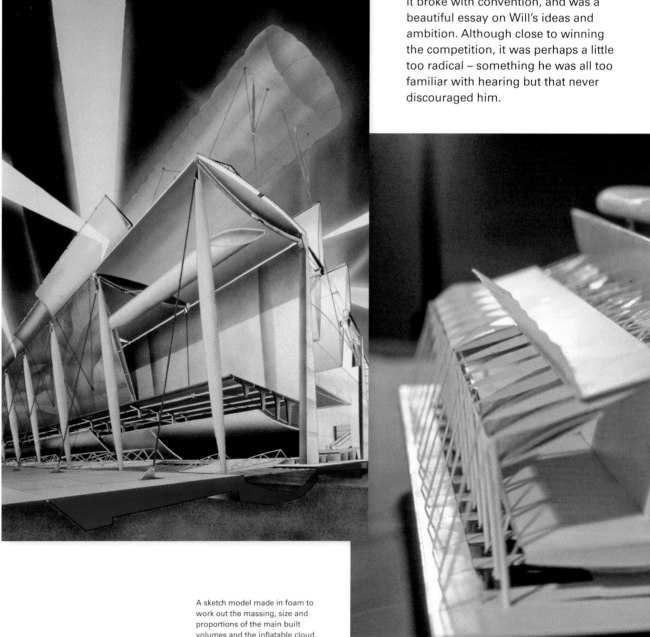

A sketch model made in foam to
work out the massing, size and
proportions of the main built
volumes and the inflatable cloud.

View from the ground looking up
to the underside of the canopy
made from a steel frame and
printed ETFE. The large nose-like
nozzle sitting inside the column is
for circulating cool air.

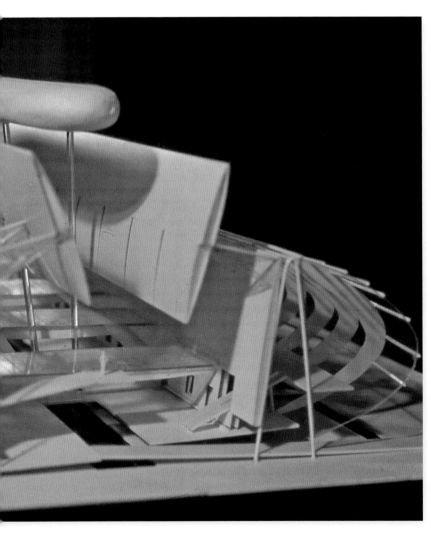

Human Comfort and Comfortingly Human

We found Will always very conscious of the environmental soundness of his buildings. We developed a proposal with him for Clarke Quay in Singapore (2006). This was a run-down area of very characterful chophouses at the edge of the marina. The idea was to upgrade the heritage buildings into high-end commercial units and add something to draw new crowds. The site had two major streets that crossed each other, and it was here that Will applied his imagination. A wholly contemporary lightweight roof covers the two streets – but the real genius is that it floats over the edge of the existing buildings without touching them, avoiding the complexity of loading and an awkward detail. The city-sized canopy serves to mediate the humid climate by controlling and suppressing the movement of air in the streets, redistributing ejected conditioned air outdoors at low levels. This improves the human comfort at ground level with a layer of cool air that would otherwise have been wastefully expelled into the atmosphere.

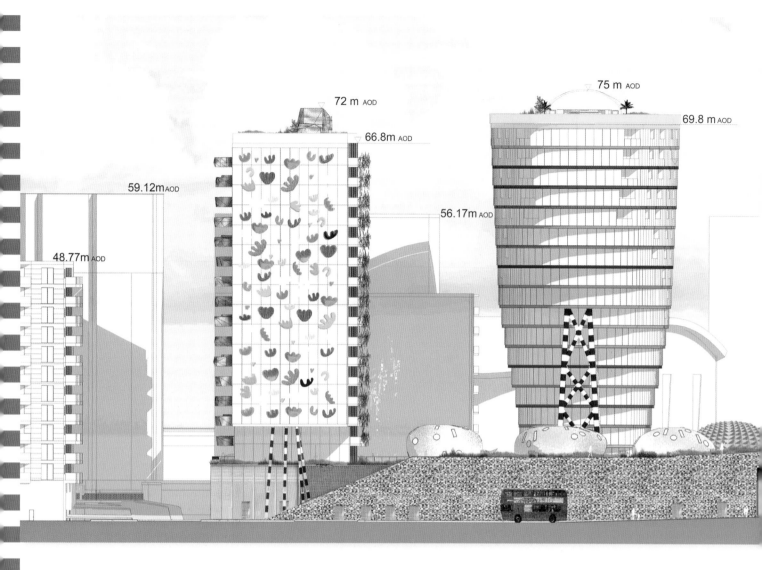

59.12m AOD

48.77m AOD

72 m AOD

66.8m AOD

56.17m AOD

75 m AOD

69.8 m AOD

aLL Design,
Kiosks and Scarves -
masterplan for Spinningfields,
Manchester, England,
2018

Digital model overview arrangement showing
the locations of proposed built interventions
for the reinvigoration of public spaces.

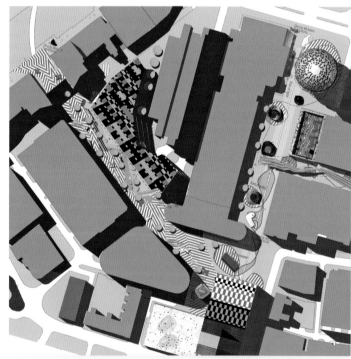

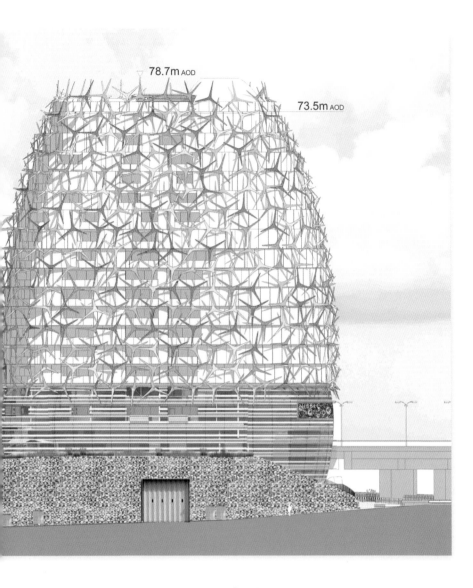

78.7m AOD

73.5m AOD

aLL Design,
Three Towers development
at Capital Interchange Way,
Brentford, London,
2014-17

General arrangement elevation for this unbuilt
scheme, showing the height of each tower, façade
treatments, and regional bus garage incorporated
at ground level, providing 60,000 square metres
(645,000 square feet) of mixed-use space.

A 2004 proposal for a rooftop extension in Shanghai; the unbuilt Three Towers development for Capital Interchange Way in Brentford, West London (2014–17); Kiosks and Scarfs (2018), a proposal to invigorate the bland public realm in Spinningfields in Manchester; and some student accommodation in Cambridge were just some of the other projects we collaborated on. The latter was sadly rejected for planning shortly after Will's death in 2018. The majority of projects we worked on together pushed the boundaries of what is recognisable in architecture. And while some of these ventures have been too extreme conceptually to be built, they were never impossible or beyond the realms of technical possibility. Will was not a man to temper his ideas and was never afraid to suggest what others might find unacceptable.

Will would often say 'Never hold onto a good idea', which on the surface seems counterintuitive, but it is a phrase that I have repeated many times as it is surprisingly liberating, at times leading to unexpected exploration in his and our work together, and in our work separately.

When David Bowie died in 2016, one of the national newspapers included the sentiment that we are all living in David Bowie's world now. On his death the huge influence Bowie had on the world was suddenly brought into focus. The same can be said of Will: we all live in Will's world now. ∆

Notes

1. See Ray Winkler and Neil Spiller (eds), ∆ *Stufish Entertainment Architecture*, November/December (no 6), 2021.
2. Neil Thomas and Aran Chadwick, *Liquid Threshold: Atelier One*, Atelier One and Actar (London and Barcelona), 2009, p 275.

While some of these ventures have been too extreme conceptually to be built, they were never impossible or beyond the realms of technical possibility

FORTY B&H AND A PORK PIE

MY DAD THE ARCHITECT

Letting us into a side of Alsop seldom seen, Will's son **Ollie Alsop** relates small vignettes of domestic and close working life, including at the family's apparently ad hoc Norfolk house. The improvised homely home seems at odds perhaps with the chimera of a successful architects' residence where material and space are held in taught alignment. Paradoxically, Will's personal habits were concerned with the exactitude of repetitively laying out his drawing, drinking and smoking accoutrements on the kitchen table each morning.

Will Alsop's family home,
Sheringham,
Norfolk, England,
1986

View from the front garden looking
towards the house. Left to right:
Sheila, Piers, Nancy and Ollie Alsop.

When I was five years old, my parents bought a house in North Norfolk in the UK, but not in the fashionable bit. More on the Martin Parr stretch of the coast – Parr being that sort of British photographer who can so skilfully capture both the joy and misery of his subjects in one snap. The house itself was ugly as hell, but it was a bargain. We went there almost every weekend, my dad driving at reckless speeds as the roads narrowed from motorway to dual carriageway and finally to single-lane. It was important to get there in three hours flat. For some reason that is what mattered. As time passed, the house evolved. There was barely a weekend when there was not some building project going on. Meanwhile, my dad was catapulted from relative obscurity to international acclaim, thanks in large part to 'Le Grand Bleu' in Marseille (1994). He became 'Will Alsop the Architect'. But when it came to the house in Norfolk, he remained curiously off-duty.

It was not a typical architect's house. Bits would be stuck onto it, then other bits would replace those bits. None of it was 'designed'. It just sort of happened. And each time we returned, there would be something new. Often it would be a surprise, including to my dad. Eventually, the work stopped, but not because it reached a natural conclusion, rather that the money ran out. To this day it has persistent issues with the plumbing, the electrics and its ability to keep the rain out, but as a family we love it. Maybe because it is the opposite of an architect's home.

The house encapsulates Will's contradictions. The location, on the periphery of polite Norfolk society, reflects a man who was on the edge of the establishment. The building itself, the result of a series of casual conversations with local builders, stands in stark contrast to the gravity-defying visions for which he was famous. He was a complex person, able to occupy dual positions on multiple fronts. He would often express a loathing of nostalgia, but he ritualistically visited the same restaurants, until the waiters no longer needed to bring the menu. He hated tradition, but at the same time he had an obsession with formal white table cloths. He was not exactly a Royalist, but he gladly accepted an OBE and quite liked the pomp that came with being a Royal Academician. He straddled different worlds, perhaps because he saw himself as an outsider.

By his own account, he had a pretty ordinary childhood in Northampton. Ordinary that is, if you ignore various bouts of pyromania including deliberately setting his twin sister's bed on fire to demonstrate the miraculous feature of 'safety' matches. Later he torched a friend's treehouse and caused an explosion in a local park after he borrowed a live grenade – a souvenir from the war – from another friend's house in order to 'test it out'. As he grew older, this sense of mischief remained, but it was accompanied by a strong determination to be successful.

It is hard to remember a time when he was not working. I would head down for breakfast in the morning to find him already at the table with his sketchbook open.

Despite having taken a solemn vow early in his life to never do any housework, his immediate vicinity at any table was the product of an obsessive-compulsive personality. All his accoutrements would be perfectly arranged. Each item set out in parallel to one another, organised like a city grid: packet of Benson and Hedges (B&H) cigarettes, cafetière coffee pot, expensive fountain pen, cheap Bic cigarette lighter, salt shaker and oversized ashtray. He would be surrounded by a thick cloud of smoke imagining amorphous shapes teetering on slender columns from the confines of a cramped dining room. In the evenings it was a similar sight, but the coffee pot would be exchanged for a wine bottle. It took regular applications of thick bleach to remove the red wine stains from the Formica table top, but the stale cigarette odour was baked in. I loved to look through his sketchbooks. They were like mini-universes. You could explore them and piece the various components together like a jigsaw. They merged life and art, juxtaposing holiday snaps next to drawings of buildings of uncertain scales. If there was no sign of him in the morning it was probably because he was on a plane. No doubt sketching at 50,000 feet.

Will Alsop,
Look, Change (detail),
date unknown

Charcoal and oil pastel depicting a desk with an open sketchbook protruding from a large rock in a forest.

Will Alsop,
Sketches for the National Literature Centre,
Swansea, Wales,
1993

One of many projects that met with opposition from local councillors and remained unbuilt.

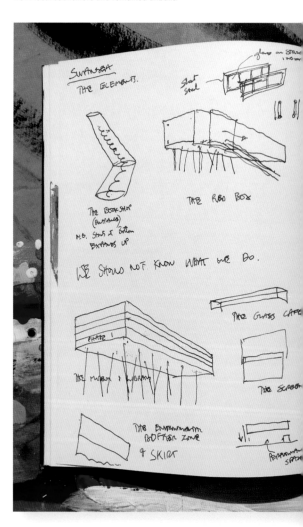

The Norfolk house in 2015

View from the street looking back towards the house. The front garden gradually became a series of rows with distinct horticultural styles and planting.

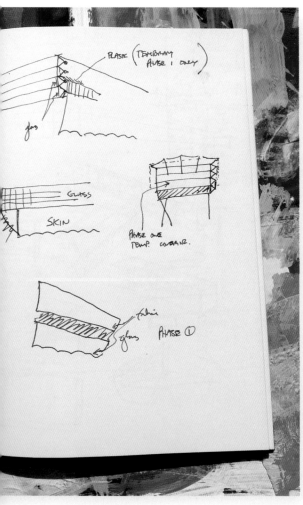

Working with Dad

Humour was a big part of his life and it played an important role in his work. It was infectious. His playfulness had a significant influence on me and my colleagues around the time when we started our digital media company Squint/Opera from a forgotten corner of my dad's Battersea studio in 2001. During those early days we would often make films about his projects for competitions or presentations. One such example, *The Birdhouse Project* (2004), was for a giant nest designed to float above the city of Osaka in Japan. We filmed him against a green screen, then digitally superimposed him onto a tangled mass of branches.

Rather than addressing the camera as himself, Will Alsop the man, he instead chose to play the role of one of the avian inhabitants, delivering an unscripted monologue that described his experience of living in the birdhouse. He touched on its value as a meeting place for socially outgoing birds and as a safe environment to rear young. Midway he paused to open a bottle of wine and smoke a cigarette. During the editing stage, we decided to overdub his voice and replace it with a nightingale's call, subtitling his spoken words. Throughout the production process, there were a number of reviews. At any point he could have pulled the plug on this obvious farce, but he never did. At the time I am not sure any of us gave it a second thought, but now I cannot help imagining how that film was received. The thought of him dimming the lights, pressing play and watching himself portray an enormous man-bird in front of his clients in an unfamiliar setting fills me with a mixture of amusement and horror. My dad would almost certainly have been unphased.

Squint/Opera,
Still from *The Birdhouse Project*,
2004

Will Alsop perches on a branch and lights a cigarette,
superimposed onto his design for a birdhouse in
Osaka, Japan.

In many of the earlier films we made of
his projects, we would include interviews
with people who would either find his
designs utterly objectionable or simply
not know what to make of them

A typical sight – in his element at the end of
the garden having escaped family duties.

Taking criticism is part of being a controversial figure. Nevertheless, not everyone can accept it in good humour. My dad certainly could not always. Yet at the same time, he did not have an overly tight grip on his self-image. I am not sure whether that was just because he could not be bothered, or whether he had done the rough calculations and worked out that in order to maintain that grip he would have to dedicate a significant proportion of his time which could be spent painting in his studio. In many of the earlier films we made of his projects, we would include interviews with people who would either find his designs utterly objectionable or simply not know what to make of them. As young filmmakers, we were often unsure whether or not these views would make the final cut, but invariably they did. Was that because he wanted to highlight those reactions as proof that he was pushing the boundaries? That the inclusion of these views was an illustration of his uncompromising vision? Or was he too busy painting to care?

My dad's ability to compartmentalise was extraordinary. When opinion turned against him, he would somehow divert all that negativity into a sort of maximum-security mind prison. His own mental Alcatraz. Stress, ill-will and failure would share a cramped cell as they served out their life sentences with no hope of parole. In his life there was no shortage of stress, much of which came from the business(es). These were massive problems – many of which were of his own making – that may have been career-ending events for those with a less robust constitution. How he managed to ride the rodeo bull from Alsop & Lyall (1980–91) to Alsop, Lyall & Störmer (1990–91), Alsop & Störmer (1991–2000), Alsop Architects (2000–06), SMC Alsop (2006–09), RMJM (2009–11) and finally to aLL Design (established in 2011) and survive is beyond me.

Squint/Opera,
Still from *Post Barnsley*,
2002

A silhouetted figure of the last postman in
Barnsley gazes over the future walled city
with a halo of light hovering above.

Will looking out from the dining room –
one of many extensions.

Since my dad's death in 2018, I have had the opportunity to organise my thoughts, but as time passes he makes less sense to me, not more. Reconciling the different sides of his character appears to me to be entirely futile

Was this ability a superpower or a symptom of psychopathy? I am not certain, but it did mean he could carry on going where others may well have given up.

The Public

Will liked straightforward, so-called 'normal' people. He often enjoyed the process of community consultation when he got to meet people from different walks of life. One such event in Barnsley, South Yorkshire at the time of his provocative 'Tuscan hill village' scheme (2002) stands out – the idea was to bulldoze the town's vast suburban sprawl and squeeze it into a 'living wall'.

The event did not take place in a grand auditorium to hundreds of people. There was no lectern. No microphone. It was not a corporate event day with everyone wearing lanyards. There were no lanyards at all. It was conducted around a table with around 15 or so members of the community. My dad was there in the room, sitting around the table not looking like a typical architect. Scruffier than you would expect. Is that red wine or paint on his shirt? His hair dangled, long and unkempt. Probably unwashed. And all the while chain smoking, pausing for the occasional glug of wine. Somehow his appearance put people at ease to discuss radical ideas. Was it the fact that he did not look like a typical architect? Rather someone you might meet in a Shell garage buying forty B&H and a pork pie.

On the flip side, he could often become exasperated by the consultative hurdles he would have to jump in order to get his schemes across the line – his patience notably short when he encountered irredeemably boring middle-management types. The sort of people who might cite clause 6.14, sub paragraph B to stifle his vision. He reserved a special hatred for the unimaginative, and his expressions of frustration could be quite public. I still remember his Stirling Prize speech, having just won the award for Peckham Library (2000) in which he announced on the podium that London's Kensington and Chelsea Borough Council go and fuck itself – its planning department had recently rejected one of his schemes for the Royal Society of British Sculptors. It was mortifying at the time. In the same way as a parent making an embarrassing scene at a restaurant. But on reflection, I miss him for his controversy.

Embracing Contradiction

Since my dad's death in 2018, I have had the opportunity to organise my thoughts, but as time passes he makes less sense to me, not more. Reconciling the different sides of his character appears to me to be entirely futile. On the one hand, he was an inspirational figure who designed impossibly strange buildings all over the world, and on the other someone who completely neglected his own domestic environment. In his heyday he was highly paid, but it made no difference because he was a complete train-wreck of a businessman whose lack of self-control left a trail of destruction in its wake. At home he was a warm and loving father, but cold-hearted business decisions sadly left various professional relationships in tatters. Coming back to the house in Norfolk, I am reminded of him. It makes no sense. It is a mess. It is a contradiction. But I will always feel a deep affection for it. ⌀

Will McLean

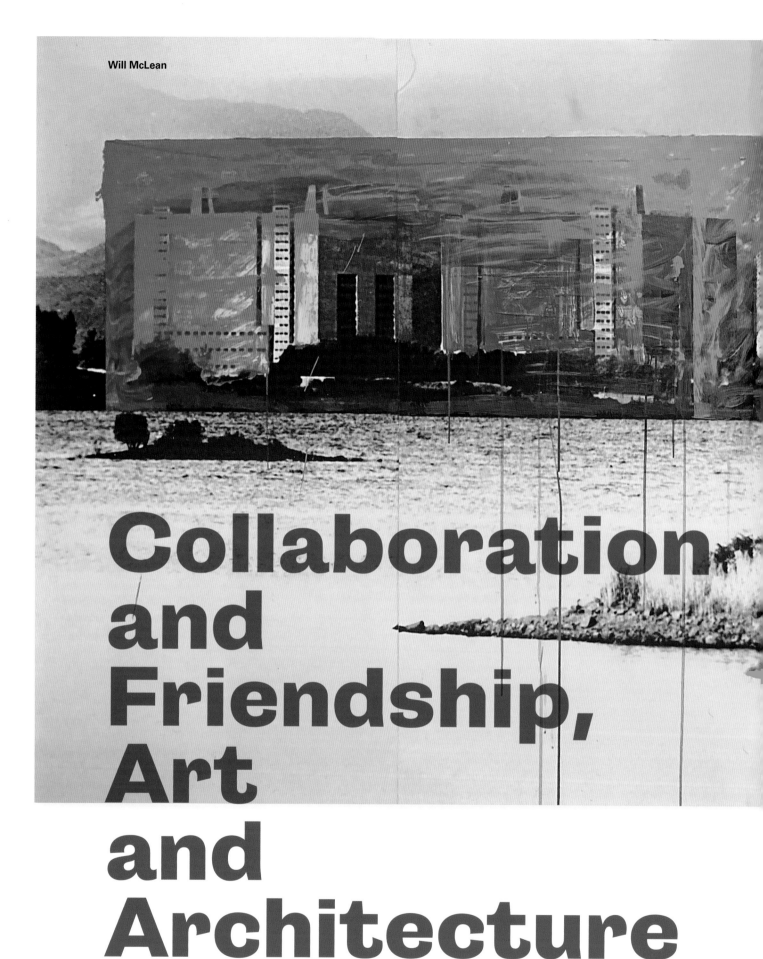

Collaboration and Friendship, Art and Architecture

Will Alsop and Bruce McLean,
Decommissioning Factory and Science Museum,
Trawsfynydd Power Station,
Wales,
1994

'Power to Change' was a televised design competition and accompanying book that
explored the closure and subsequent decommissioning process of one of the UK's
first nuclear power-stations. As one of four invited international teams, Alsop, McLean,
Mel Gooding, David Gothard and structural engineer Matthew Wells devised a novel
approach that would celebrate, explain and visualise this dangerous and lengthy
process and become a worldwide learning centre for nuclear decommissioning.

Will McLean discusses the close bond and respect between his artist father Bruce McLean and Will Alsop, and shares insights into some of their important collaborations. Will McLean had worked as a teenager in Alsop's office, was inspired by him to study at the Architectural Association and subsequently worked on a number of key office projects in the 1990s. He observed first-hand the creative ethos and free-ranging discipline that his father and Alsop worked relentlessly – and with unfailing good-humour – to materialise in projects for buildings, paintings and products.

I liked working with him, knowing that nothing would ever get built, but then it would sometimes.
— Bruce McLean (2022)

Will Alsop and Bruce McLean in Bilbao for the architecture workshop 'Placa to Placa', 2006

Alsop and McLean led an open student workshop rethinking the whole of Bilbao in relation to the river Nervión that runs through the city.

Will Alsop and Bruce McLean were friends. McLean reflects that 'he didn't seem like a typical architect, but I'm not a typical artist'. Prior to his architectural studies, Alsop had studied at Northampton Art School (1964–66), and McLean's father was an architect and partner in the eminent Glasgow firm Gratton and McLean – so they understood each other's worlds. Art and Architecture had become a very popular movement in the early 1970s but had failed, in Alsop's view, because it became 'managed' by consultants who did not understand that any union for a project must firstly be rooted in mutual respect and, more importantly, friendship.

Bruce McLean studied sculpture at Saint Martin's School of Art in London (1963–6) and has gone on to make paintings, performances, ceramics, buildings and films but all under the guise of sculpture. He believes that you cannot be an architect if you are not an artist, and references a lecture given at the Slade School of Art in London by artist Gary Woodley in the 1990s, entitled 'Can bad sculptors make good architects?'. McLean says the answer is yes, and he mentions Erwin Heerich (1922–2004) and Fritz Wotruba (1907–75) as chief proponents of this specific art. He has collaborated with a number of architects including David Chipperfield (Arnolfini Bar, Bristol, 1987) and Nigel Coates (Kinetic Painting for disco), in collaboration with Branson Coates Architects, Tokyo, 1989), but it was his working relationship and friendship with Will Alsop that endured and best encapsulates the collaborative potential of these two arts (and artists).

The Art Centre
Alsop and McLean first met at Riverside Studios in Hammersmith, London, in 1979 – in the bar. The original Riverside Studios was an art centre comprising artist studios, performance spaces, a gallery, bar and bookshop (1976–2014). Assistant director and chief organisational protagonist at Riverside at the time was David Gothard who attracted a staggering line-up of radical and experimental international visitors to this local art centre, including

writer Kathy Acker, choreographer Trisha Brown, writer Samuel Beckett and musician Laurie Anderson, as well as supporting emerging talent such as dancer Michael Clark and playwright Hanif Kureishi. McLean was painting in a studio there and Alsop and John Lyall had an office at the back of the building. The bar was the focal point of Riverside when it opened each evening at 6pm (there was no view or access to the actual riverside as Alsop pointed out) – and it was the time when many people working in the building and visitors for shows and events would gather, meet and talk to each other.

In November 1979, McLean and Paul Richards staged and performed *The Masterwork*, a multi-headed performance artwork, at Riverside, with a musical score by Michael Nyman. Programmed as the 'definitive work in mediocrity', it was subtitled *An Award Winning Fishknife* and was a highly choreographed and scabrous tale about an architect whose major coup de grâce was the development of some over-designed tableware. McLean had asked Alsop to design the costumes, which was their first, but tentative, collaboration. McLean remembers that they featured reflective hi-vis strips – echoes of the safety clothing that Alsop had designed while working for Cedric Price on his McAppy (1974–5) project for good labour relations and site safety undertaken for family construction firm Robert McAlpine and Sons.

In 1984 McLean and art critic Mel Gooding had started to devise a plan for the Mortlake Palace of Contemporary Arts, right next to the River Thames in Southwest London,[1] a self-initiated venture on the site of a brewery close to McLean's home about half a mile away. With the help and support of local business-management consultant Roger Poulet and Nicholas Serota, then director of the Whitechapel Gallery, they approached the local authority and the brewery owners with a feasibility study. They had also approached Alsop for his architectural input and this was the start of a working relationship, albeit quite a formal arrangement. The Mortlake Palace was never built, but its high ambitions for the conversion of vast industrial buildings with contemporary additions, and an 'art bus route' through London, were not only influential (think a proto-Tate Modern (2000), a project Serota was instrumental in realising), but also embodied many of the architectural influences that McLean and Alsop were bringing to the table, such as Cedric Price's Fun Palace (1960) and InK, the Hallen für Internationale Neue Kunst, Zurich (1978–81).

Bruce McLean and Will Alsop,
Mortlake Palace of Contemporary Arts,
Mortlake,
London,
1984

Devised by McLean, Alsop and colleague Mel Gooding, the Mortlake Palace of Contemporary Arts was a speculative proposal to turn part of a large brewery site in Southwest London into an international arts venue. The proposal would have seen the selective reuse of existing structures as well as new purpose-built facilities. Note the reference to 'Will's Knotted Hanky' – Alsop's roof idea indicated at the top of the drawing.

Working Drawings

It was not until 1986 that Alsop and McLean actually collaborated on the same painting. Alsop stated that it was only a matter of time before they got together in his studio to paint together, which was usually on a large scale, and always on paper. What Alsop liked was that these collaborations were explorations, not artworks. This work was what might now be described as research; not a term either Alsop or McLean liked or would use. Alsop had already observed and learnt from the artist that the act of painting was not a precious activity and the decision to paint on paper and not canvas was conscious – these were works-in-progress and part of an ongoing conversation.

Likewise, McLean learnt from Alsop to quickly move on from the crushing defeat of an architectural competition, lost, or even won (and then lost). Seldom visibly down-hearted, Alsop appeared to embrace the next project with renewed enthusiasm and ambition. When they were having a conversation and McLean came up with a notion, Alsop would never dismiss it; he may not have used it, but nothing was ever dismissed or discarded out of hand. McLean, Alsop and Gooding met frequently in the evening and it was these discussions and conversational meanderings that were the basis of both friendship and work. Gooding once remarked (laughing) that 'Alsop would steal or borrow any idea he could lay his brain on'. Alsop reflected on those evenings that it was the excitement of the possibility of seeing something new that was the crux

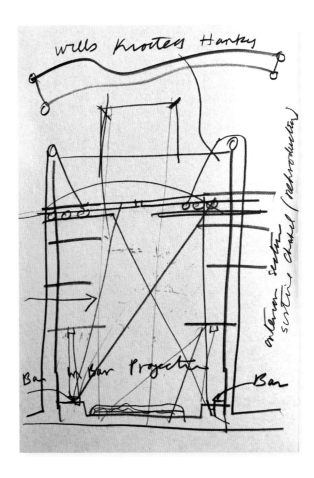

of the meetings – 'you could retreat to your bed feeling something had been achieved and in the morning it was forgotten, it did not matter'.[2]

Alsop considered these conversations and collaborations as an essential adjunct to the day job. His parents would always play bridge on a Tuesday evening, and Alsop and McLean could see no reason why they should not always paint on a Tuesday evening, so they did. Making a decision to paint and draw was the point. Content would emerge out of that process and Alsop valued it greatly: 'This process has informed my architectural practice and has led to working closely with the general public in order to discover something. Design, as indeed painting, is a voyage of discovery.'[3]

Malagarba Works

In 1990, Alsop visited McLean at his studio on the Balearic island of Menorca. They worked on the beginnings of an architectural competition for Potsdamer Platz in Berlin. Alsop's practice, Alsop, Lyall & Störmer, had been invited to make an entry for the re-planning of this flattened area of the city, which was deeply imbued with historic significance. Undaunted, they embarked on a series of paintings and drawings that formed the basis of the competition submission. This became the first of many visits to Menorca which resulted in the books *City of Objects: Designs on Berlin* (1992)[4] and *Malagarba Works* (2003)[5] – the latter being the most comprehensive record of Alsop and McLean's collaborative works, and covering a period of exploration that took their ideas to a new dimension.

Malagarba is the name of the piece of untamed, untethered rural land where the studio is based, characterised by low dry vegetation, rocks, big cactuses and the odd lizard. The typical day was divided. Menorca in the summer is more than warm after 10.30am, and so Alsop and McLean would start work at 7am and continue until breakfast at 11am, then rest and reconvene at 'gin-and-tonic hour' until the light faded. That first year they needed a sheet of plywood. This necessitated them carrying a large board through the streets of the tiny village of Es Migjorn Gran up the hill to the studio. McLean remarked at the time that he could not imagine Richard Rogers and Anthony Caro doing the same! Their collaborations involved the menial, which Alsop considered to be meaningful. The work done at *Malagarba* could be described as pure luxury in the sense there were no deadlines, clients or phones. They were free to do anything that might, or might not, feed the projects that occupied their day-to-day working lives. Alsop latterly reflected that he could see that the *Malagarba* works were 'normal life' and everything else a distraction.[6] They did not make art – they observed, they made, they built, they tested, they sweated, they laughed and tested again.

These heated experiments reached their apotheosis at the 2003 Valencia Biennale: The Ideal City, where Alsop and McLean collaboratively designed the *A&M – Department of Proper Behaviour* installation. The project was a department store of art, architecture and experience featuring a bar designed by McLean and staffed by Menorcan friend

Will Alsop and Bruce McLean, Competition paintings for Potsdamer Platz, Berlin, 1991

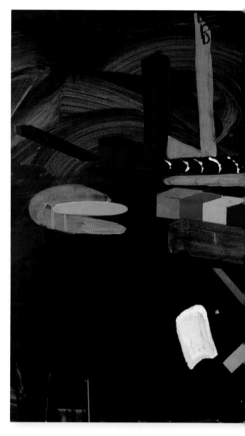

right: The city of Berlin invited 17 practices including Alsop, Lyall & Störmer to submit proposals for the redevelopment of Potsdamer Platz and the surrounding area, which had been largely destroyed in the Second World War.

below: The buildings consisted of a group of L-shaped megastructures including offices and corporate headquarters radiating from Potsdamer Platz station and lifted off the ground.

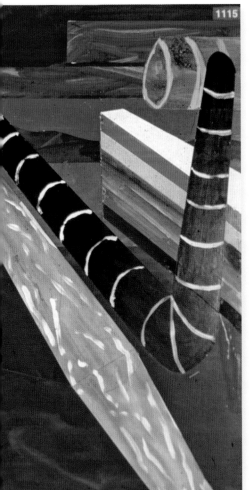

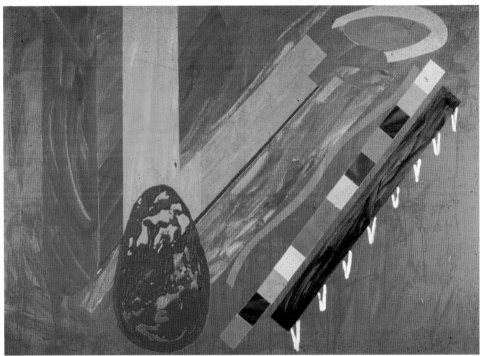

above: By elevating the blocks, a massive landscape garden was created at ground level, part of a larger environmental strategy for the natural heating and cooling of the structures devised by Chris McCarthy and Guy Battle.

At the core, for artist and architect, lies a relentless pursuit of style and beauty to lift the human spirit which came quite naturally, but with a lot of hard work, to them both

and artist Bep Gomilla. This perfectly ephemeral bar, not designed to last, was an environment where the performance of the perfectly timed drink and the carefully placed snack created a theatre of mannerism, gesture and performance in what Alsop described as a 'celebration of everything you normally do'.[7]

Commissions and Decommissions

The future decommissioning of Trawsfynydd nuclear power-station in North Wales (1994) was one of the more unusual invited architectural competitions that the duo put their minds to. Teaming up again with Gooding, they devised a plan – 'Knowledge = Power' – that would not hide or disguise the dangerous and lengthy decommissioning process, but would literally illuminate this facility as a new international centre of knowledge and research on

safely transforming, decontaminating and remediating the site. Gooding composed a poem and Alsop and McLean produced large-scale paintings and collages. The competition was filmed for a BBC television programme entitled 'Power to Change',[8] and an accompanying book of the same name was produced, documenting the entries and history of the site.

But do not be mistaken, the musings were not without application; the experimentation fed directly into major building projects featured in the mix with an early collaboration at Tottenham Hale Railway Station (Alsop, Lyall & Störmer, London, 1992) where McLean had replaced (like for like) what would have been a series of clear glazed panels on a station platform with a 53-metre (174-foot) long painting on enamelled steel panels – 'a rare example of art which is an essential part of the architecture and not a decorative afterthought'.[9] This approach was echoed by integration of the external glazing of the Blizard building housing the London School of Medicine and Dentistry for Queen Mary University at its Whitechapel campus (2005), and Finch West subway station in Toronto, Canada (2018).

As a young student of architecture and as a practice employee at Alsop, Lyall & Störmer (1985–94), I helped out in making, among other things, the model for the Potsdamer Platz competition and the competition model for Tate Modern – the latter so large I could build it from the inside out. Alsop was convinced that he was going to win that competition, and when he did not even get short-listed, he just got on with the next project. The office motto was 'no style, no beauty', which would brilliantly wind up the architecture lovers, the taste-makers and the profession. In this respect, Alsop was most certainly the pupil of Cedric Price – the self-styled 'conscience of the profession'[10] – and found comradeship with McLean whose individual work is expressed in many different mediums. At the core, for artist and architect, lies a relentless pursuit of style and beauty to lift the human spirit which came quite naturally, but with a lot of hard work, to them both. ⌂

This article is based on an interview with Bruce McLean in London, January 2022.

Notes
1. Samantha Hardingham (ed), *Experiments in Architecture,* August (London), 2005, pp 68–81.
2. Taken from 'Bruce', an unpublished contribution by Will Alsop for a future book on the work of Bruce McLean. Received by Will McLean, March, 2016.
3. *Ibid.*
4. Will Alsop, Bruce McLean and Jan Störmer, *City of Objects: Designs on Berlin*, Ellipsis (London), 1992.
5. Bruce McLean and Will Alsop, *Malagarba Works*, John Wiley & Sons (London), 2003.
6. *Ibid.*
7. Will McLean, 'Celebrate Everything You Normally Do: Will Alsop's Praxis', *Corridor 8: Visual Art in the Supercity of Will Alsop*, Michael Butterworth (Manchester), 2009, pp 4–7.
8. David Barrie (ed), *Power to Change: Architecture for a New Age of Nuclear Waste and Decommissioning*, BBC (Wales), 1995, pp 44–55.
9. Samantha Hardingham, *London: A Guide to Recent Architecture*, Ellipsis (London), 1993, p 226.
10. Samantha Hardingham, *Cedric Price Works 1952–2003: A Forward-Minded Retrospective*, AA Publications/CCA (London), 2016, p 306.

Clare Hamman

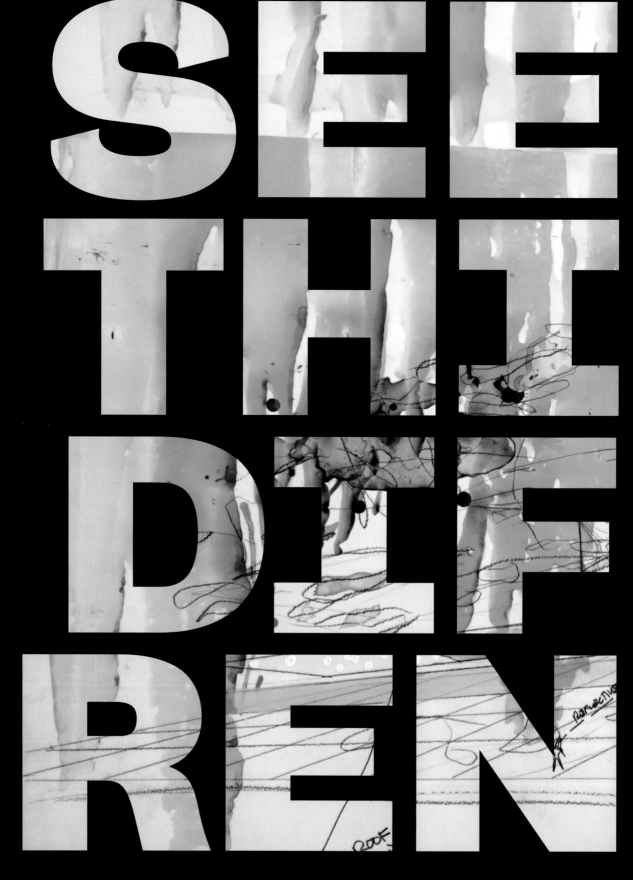

SEE
THI
DIF
REN

PAINTING, THE OBJECT AND

THE ART OF CONVERSATION

Clare Hamman gives us a peek into the impressive collection of Alsop paintings held by the Marco Goldschmeid Foundation, and ruminates on the applications for which Alsop used his painterly instincts. Firstly, this was to clear his own mind of preconceived ideas, then, as a catalyst for creativity in his office and with collaborators, as well as a prompt for open-minded discussion with clients. Hamman positions the role of painting in Alsop's design practice as both a life-giving force and powerful means of popular communication.

Will Alsop,
Le Grand Bleu,
1990

Early competition paintings for the Hôtel du Département des Bouches-du-Rhône in Marseille, which was completed in 1994, did not feature the colour for which 'Le Grand Bleu' building is better known.

The year after Will Alsop completed Cardiff Bay Visitor Centre in Wales (1990), he reflected on how describing it as a building was constrictive. Loaded with connotations of brick and concrete, he felt the word 'building' narrowed the possibilities of what architecture could be. Instead, he preferred to use the term 'object', drawing connections to sculpture and releasing projects from the assumptions of conventional building; from having to 'conform to all the expectations the name suggests'.[1] Escaping expectations was Alsop's modus operandi, and painting sat at the heart of his working method to achieve this. Developed throughout his career, his expressive language of painting enabled him to explore and question the potential of what architecture is, and create a vocabulary for that conversation.

Painting as Process

1990 was also the year that heralded him winning the competition to build the Hôtel du Département des Bouches-du-Rhône (1994), Marseille's new regional government headquarters, famously beating Norman Foster into second place. The experimental complex with its memorable 'X' column structure sits astride the Metro line with the Mediterranean Sea in sight. Entering the building through sliding doors between the Xs, the generous atrium arches overhead; a publicly accessible, almost clinical space, bridging the span between two private administrative blocks. Shading strategies were incorporated as part of the design against the unrelenting Mediterranean sun, while the profile of the external forms was refined and an aerofoil added to the council chamber block to protect pedestrians from the strong mistral wind. The cool, considered white interior emulates the care given to the building's environmental response but belies the exterior hue; the brilliant Yves Klein of the external skin, created in collaboration with artist Brian Clarke, which lends the building its moniker of 'Le Grand Bleu'.

Alsop's paintings were fundamental to the project. They were a key design tool for him and colleagues in the office as they stepped through the stages of the competition, honing their design proposal. Where sketches were informative, the paintings captured the spirit of the building and how it could instigate the revitalisation of a deprived quartier to the north of the historic city of Marseille. But they also formed part of Alsop's showmanship in the final stages of the competition when he produced a couple of canvases with a flourish and gifted them to the client.

This was not the first time that Alsop had used paintings as part of a client presentation. Whether abstract or illustrative, the paintings opened up the possibility of conversation and debate with the client as they 'didn't feel threatened by the paintings'.[2] An intricate technical drawing may demonstrate authority, but it is also difficult for the audience to criticise. Conversely, the fluidity of the paintings encouraged discussion of the idea itself, engaging everyone in the process of design.

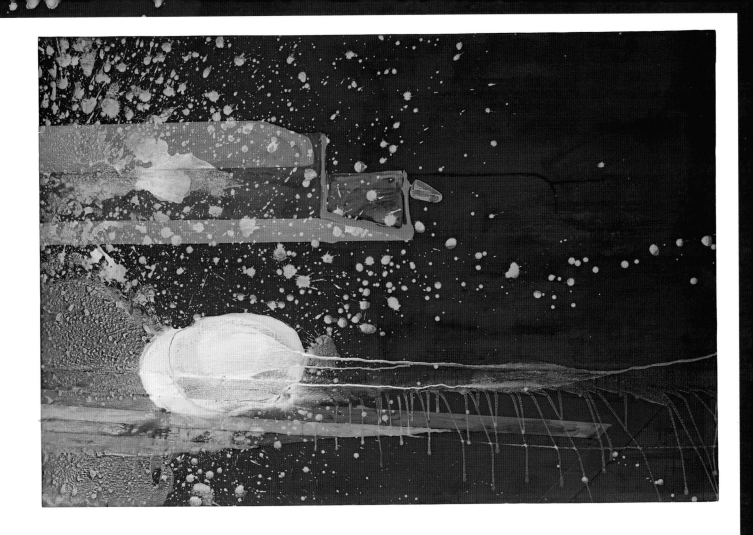

Will Alsop,
Untitled,
1999

above: Alsop's paintings are
not always explicitly related
to a project, but resonate with
ideas reminiscent of other
projects he was working on.

Will Alsop,
Garden of the Boroughs,
London,
1998

*right (and detail on previous
spread):* Adding colour drew
attention to elements of
the sketch, helping Alsop
and his colleagues to work
through different stages
of design development.

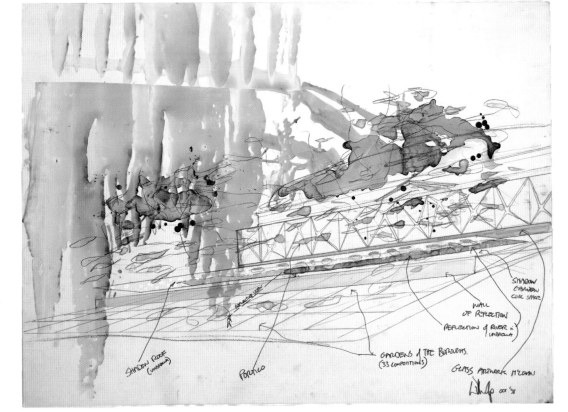

Will Alsop,
Nantes,
1990

One of six designs for 'boxes of delight' – mobile art galleries proposed for the Nantes Art Gallery competition that would move around the city – here shown with piloti to walk around on, recalling the work of Archigram.

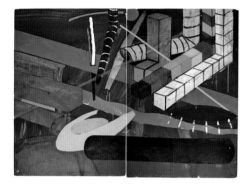

Will Alsop and Bruce McLean,
Potsdamer Platz,
1992

Potsdamer Platz had been bisected by the Berlin Wall for 20 years. Alsop was invited to participate in the competition to transform the vast, empty site at the centre of Berlin into a new business district. He and McLean envisaged a 'City of Objects', allowing the city's landscape to flow between and around the building 'objects', echoing the levelled bomb sites found across the city, but in contradiction to the divide imposed by the Wall.

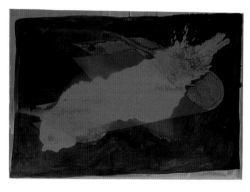

Will Alsop,
Untitled (Umwelt Behörde),
1993

Alsop not only used paintings to depict the form of a new proposal, but to also suggest the character it may embody. Here, the fluid atmosphere of the proposed Umwelt Behörde (Environment Agency) building for Hamburg, Germany, is captured, alluding to the layered interplay of elements such as the garden atrium with the structure and façade.

Imaginative Explorations

Despite his art school education, Alsop did not begin to use painting within the context of his architecture until the 1980s. Rarely done at either of the first two London offices in Hammersmith's Riverside Studios, or the Power House in Chelsea, he instead painted at home in Norfolk or with his great friend Bruce McLean. Later offices in Parkgate Studios in Battersea, South London, and Vyner Street in East London incorporated larger painting spaces.

Alsop met sculptor McLean at Riverside Studios in 1979 at a time when McLean was experimenting with paint and drawing. Alsop was attracted to the possibilities of these methods, learning to give the materials space and riffing on the outcomes. Initially coming to their painting sessions with ideas jotted in a notebook, Alsop learnt over time to be present to the process of painting and the serendipity it might create. Reflecting on these early days, McLean described how the sploshing of paint and the pair's detached conversation had affected Alsop: it 'ventilated him; aerated his whole work. It's not earthbound, but light. Heavyweight but airy.'[3]

This idea of light and airy architecture is obvious in Alsop's piloti-lifted structures – not just the X-columns of 'Le Grand Bleu', but also in later works such as Peckham Library, London (2000), and taken to an extreme at the Sharpe Centre for Design at the Ontario College of Art & Design (OCAD) in Toronto (2004), the bulk of the art college soaring above the existing buildings. But it was there in subtler ways too in earlier projects, such as the collaboration between McLean and Alsop on the competition to re-create Berlin's Potsdamer Platz (1992). Recognising the destruction and division the city had suffered, they used it as an opportunity to imagine a different sort of city – a city of objects where buildings would be placed in seemingly random configurations, some horizontal, others vertical, many cantilevered above the ground plane. Consciously occupying three dimensions, the streets flowed between, beneath and around the sculptural forms, giving the city back to the citizens.

One can read a lot about Alsop's working methods by looking at the paintings themselves. Some are very rapid, little more than sketches, the paint appearing only just to catch the idea passing through his mind. Others are heavily annotated, processing ideas and working through options, pushing what might be possible beyond the obvious conclusion. Others still capture a mood, an intention of space, to be read as the depiction of an atmosphere rather than a figurative representation. These would usually be created alone then shown to colleagues, collaborators and clients to start a conversation or push it in another direction. The Potsdamer artworks are, however, different, with the artists working together on the same pieces. These experimental, jazz-like refrains stand in stark contrast to Alsop's early foundation at art school in Northampton (1964–66) where, under the keen eye of artist Henry Bird (1909–2000) he had to draw a brick repeatedly, learning how to achieve the ultimate economy of line. The discipline of looking was key, representing the brick in its true proportions, not distracting with shading.[4]

The process of repetition instils a muscle memory within one's hands, freeing the brain from the detail of drawing and allowing it to create connections between the current moment and the broader ideas beyond the page. Alsop took this a stage further during the early years of his working career when he challenged himself to design a building a day, reasoning that just as one can only become a world-class tennis player by constant practice, the same must be true of a designer.[5]

Bridges of Conversation

In the mid-1990s, Alsop returned to Northampton, the town of his birth, to create a masterplan to revitalise the River Nene and link the former industrial area of Blackmills to Northampton town centre. Imagining the river as a 'Cultural Mile', the Millennium Park scheme (1995–7) optimised it 'as a resource for leisure and public transport'.[6] The idea of a series of bridges was developed, physically connecting the banks while alluding to historical and cultural seams underpinning the town; an Art Bridge housing a gallery, the Shoemaker's Bridge for the town's manufacturing heritage, a Swimmers Bridge imagining people using the river for recreaton while appreciating the parkland. Rather than dictating the form the redeveloped landscape would take, Alsop's series of strongly coloured graphic paintings, overlaid with vinyl lettering, suggested the ambience that could be created for and by the people by transforming this disused land.

Alsop's desire to challenge and provoke, pushing ideas another step further, was evident in another bridge. In 1995 he designed a scheme for a new gallery and headquarters for the Institute of Contemporary Arts (ICA) in London, envisaging a gallery that would utilise the piers of the former London-to-Chatham railway that cross the River Thames alongside Blackfriars Bridge. The supporting elements to the multi-arts centre – restaurants and offices, shops and bars – would span the river, forming a physical support to what Alsop described as 'boxes of delight', kinetic galleries mounted on rails that could be moved between the north and south banks of the river as desired; singular spaces or joined together to create an infinitely flexible exhibition space.[7] There are clear resonances here to Alsop's former tutor and mentor Cedric Price's Fun Palace (1961): its adaptability, its engagement with disused structure, but most obviously its celebration of joy.[8]

Disordering Device

Where the discipline Alsop found in the repetition of daily design practice helped him to explore architecture in one direction, the painting – sploshing and experimental, measured and intentional – expanded ideas on a different plane. Interviewed in 1992 by architectural journalist and editor Paul Finch, Alsop reflected on the true benefit of the paintings. As objects, they demonstrated themselves to be a valuable 'tool for opening up a conversation with the client', but the practice of creating the paintings was ultimately 'a tool to develop a conversation with yourself'.[9]

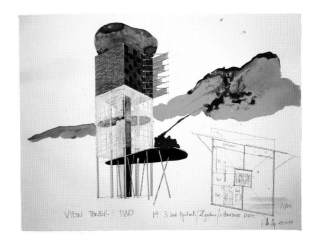

Will Alsop,
View Tower Two,
1997

Sketches helped Alsop to work through potential building elements and layouts of plans. They also captured possible colours and an overall design approach.

Will Alsop,
The Swimmers Bridge,
1996

One of six bridge paintings created with local artist Malcolm Pollard for the proposed Millennium Park scheme for Northampton, England (1995–7). The paintings invite people to engage in the playful possibility of how a new park could transform the landscape and be inhabited by visitors.

Will Alsop,
Multi-modal crossing of Thames at Blackfriars,
1995

Alsop designed two schemes in 1995 for inhabited bridges that would cross the River Thames at Blackfriars, London – the realised Blackfriars station, and the proposal for the Institute of Contemporary Arts (ICA). This early painting imagines how three bridges would sit together: the station would inhabit the railway bridge; cars would be prohibited from the existing road bridge; and, sandwiched between the two on the disused 19th-century bridge piers would be the slice of culture offered by the ICA.

Will Alsop,
River of Dreams,
1997

In his entry for the Clyde Weir Competition,
Glasgow, Scotland (1997), Alsop proposed a strategic
redevelopment of the River Clyde from its famous
industrial base to reframe it as the city's cultural centre.
Conceived as a series of dancing forms across the river,
the scheme included an aquarium, museum, climbing
wall, student accommodation and a 'Wall of Dance'.

This internal conversation preceded all of the others. Art historian Mel Gooding described it as Alsop's methodology; to reach a moment of clarity removed from thought. What emerges are 'imaginative explorations in visual terms of the experience of buildings'.[10] Within these layers of experience are the echoes of creative conversations Alsop had across the decades with tutors, friends, colleagues and partners. But perhaps most significantly, the paintings opened a dialogue with the public – the people who would ultimately use the proposed buildings, engaging a different perspective. The paintings offered bridges to challenge and provoke the tacit lines of convention within architecture, planning and society at large. Why should a building not sit delicately above its neighbours? Or be moveable?

BEYOND THE MILLENNIUM – RIVER J DREAMS

In Responsibilities Begin Dreams

Knowing how painting had helped him, in 2013 Alsop ran mentoring sessions with A-Level students considering a career in architecture. Held at the Royal Academy of Arts in London, a dozen students painted a billboard-sized canvas, stretching the length of the room. Encouraging experimentation, play and mess, Alsop urged his collaborators to keep working at the painting with a high degree of intensity until you see something: 'the most important thing is to do it, and to do it with some sort of energy.'[11]

Just as the paintings prompted conversations for Alsop, they are finding a new voice through the Alsop collection of paintings held by the Marco Goldschmied Foundation (MGF). Spanning more than 20 years, it is an eclectic mix of artworks, some titled to a particular project, others visually related, and all part of an ongoing conversation beyond convention. From large, deliberate canvases to sketches on scraps of tracing paper, some framed for display, others stashed in portfolios, the sheets adhering to each other when the ink was not yet dry. What is evident from them all is Alsop's energy of creation, the same energy he encouraged in the A-Level students; grabbing whatever materials were close to hand to capture a fleeting idea, ready to be reapproached, askance, to evolve into the next iteration.

Whilst future voices in architecture will inevitably look to Alsop's built and unbuilt projects for inspiration, they must also look to his paintings as a source of ongoing creative dialogue. Two decades after Alsop's Peckham Library won the Stirling Prize, Marco Goldschmied announced the MGF's ambition to sponsor a new bursary award at the London School of Architecture (LSA). Since 1998, the MGF has sponsored the Stephen Lawrence Prize and offered bursaries to support students through the long years of study. The new bursary will build on this reputation and Alsop's drive to support and encourage creativity in students. Will Alsop understood the importance of a polyphony of voices to create a rich urban environment; the MGF wants to ensure it remains possible. ⚙

Notes
1. 'The Late Show', BBC Two, 4 March 1991.
2. *Ibid.*
3. *Ibid.*
4. Will Alsop, 'Drawing on the Experiences of Life Help [sic] Create Better Work', *Architects' Journal*, 213 (25), 28 June 2001, p 16.
5. 'Third Ear', BBC Radio 3, 19 May 1992.
6. Stephen Dobney (ed), *Alsop & Störmer: Selected and Current Works*, Images Publishing Group (Mulgrave, VIC), 1999, p 133.
7. Mel Gooding, 'A River Runs Through It', *Independent*, 25 June 1995: www.independent.co.uk/arts-entertainment/art/news/a-river-runs-through-it-1588364.html.
8. Canadian Centre for Architecture (CCA), 'Fun Palace Project': www.cca.qc.ca/en/archives/380477/cedric-price-fonds/396839/projects/399301/fun-palace-project#fa-obj-310196.
9. 'Third Ear', *op cit.*
10. 'The Late Show', *op cit.*
11. Royal Academy of Arts, 'Will Alsop RA (1947–2018)': www.royalacademy.org.uk/art-artists/name/will-alsop-ra.

The Wills of Words

Mark Garcia

Will Alsop's home office,
Sheringham, Norfolk,
2021

Will collected and absorbed a significant library of thousands of books and documents, articles and essays. Many of these would contain work about or for actual issues of △.

An Allsop Mediagraphy

'Architects ... usually their thoughts and theories fail and, after causing a lot of stress, get knocked down ... As I get older I have developed a deep distrust of architectural theory.'

— Will Alsop, 2011 [1]

There were many Alsops: painter, sculptor, writer, impresario and lecturer/design tutor. **Mark Garcia** discusses the chameleon aspects of Alsop's oeuvre and his attitude to architectural theory. He tries to unravel these renegade 'Wills' and ultimately celebrates the dexterity of Alsop's thought patterns and creative output.

Is a theory of 'Will Alsop' desirable or even possible? If not theory, then do Alsopesque non-theory theories exist, or are these just Willian ideas and ideations? The man himself would have said no to the first and second and agreed on the third count. But therein lies the problem: there are so many Wills – Alsop the architect, the painter, the public and media intellectual, W. Alsop the author of multiple books, the journalist, the writer and, my favourite, the raconteur. But where is Will the critic, theorist and philosopher – did/does he even exist? All of these wills of Wills overlap, none are quite identical, all are interesting.

The dilemma is that the Wills changed their mind about these things. In his book *Will Alsop: The Noise* (2011), Tom Porter quotes Alsop's statement about his own (but not others') theory, noting that it was healthy that we now lived in an age of '"post-theory" (if only)' and that: 'In my 20s I was full of philosophy, which I downgraded to theory when I was 30 ... When I was 40, this became downgraded to concept ... when I was 50, it became idea ... now I'm 60 it's become just a notion. When I reach 70, I hope I have no fucking idea.'[2]

But the evidence is more ambiguous. The sites and primary textual and written evidence of criticism, history, theory and philosophy (let's just call these 'writings/texts/words' and 'ideas' for now) in Alsop's polymorphous oeuvre are extensive. His written items (whether published and publicly accessible or privately stored on hard-drives, on buildings, in artworks, in documented workshops and events, painted or scribbled in notebooks or on scraps of paper) can be considered separately as a significant and living literary legacy to architectural and design text-art and art-texts, as well as in the context of his whole and evolving body of non-textual/written ideas and ideation.

Will Alsop's home office, Sheringham, Norfolk, 2021

Evidence of the 460 or so books, essays and articles written about him and over 60 written by him is contained in this pair of photographs of the two loft sides of Will's desk/library/office, the source of many of the 'words of the Wills', at his Sheringham home.

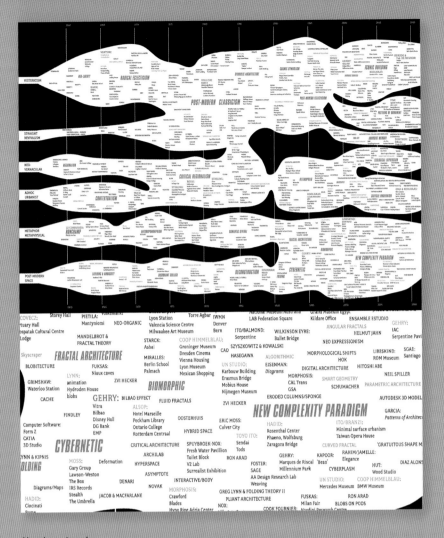

Charles Jencks,
'A Sea Of Many Streams',
2010

In the roll-call of Jencks's lionising, pluralising diagram-icon of 20th–21st-century architectural canons, Alsop's relative position can be seen in the close-up detail, at the confluence of the 'Metaphor Metaphysical' and 'Post-Modern Space' streams, caught between 'Fractal Architecture', 'Biomorphic', 'Cybernetic' and 'New Complexity Paradigm'. The list of his representative works features his Marseille, Peckham, OCAD and Rotterdam Centraal buildings.

Rather than 'theory/theories', Will preferred to refer to these sorts of things as more personal and individual 'interests', 'concerns' and 'curiosities'. What if any clear ideas that cut through the oeuvre are there? The difficulty here lies in the synthesis required, because Alsop's ideas and theories are diffused and fragmented throughout the multimedia primary sources, sites and spaces of his words/texts/writings but also those about him and his works (written or otherwise). Where did the spaces of Alsop's writings, artworks and architecture begin, occur and meld? On, in, around and through the designed spaces of his desks, offices and studios, is one answer.

For the polymath Charles Jencks, Alsop was an architect of icons and gains his place in the 2010 version of Jencks's 'A Sea of Many Streams' – his auto-iconic evolutionary diagram of architectures (first edition, 1995). I would position a Will in the 'Critical Regionalism', 'Heteropolis', 'Ad Hocist Memory', 'Time City', 'Patterns Of Ornament', 'Iconic Building', 'Enigmatic Signifier' and 'Post-Modern Eclecticism' sections of this diagram. Being prolific (having built for more than 40 years), diverse and mercurial, no one singular or simplistic category can contain all the Wills, so Alsop should manifest as more of a plural, distributed and multi-style/anti-style/no-style genre-scribble, an across-the-board and 21st-century phenomenon reaching far into the future.

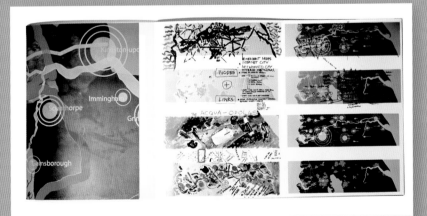

Will Alsop and James Hulme,
Will Alsop's SuperCity,
2005

Inside covers and frontispiece diagrams. Once called 'gesamtkunstwerks' and now 'transmedia' or 'multimedia', Alsop's most memorable contribution to this rare type was 'Supercity UK' (2004–18), an exhibition, installation, TV series, book and a short story, a form which would in 2014 become the novel in *Las Heras*.

Alsop's Architexts

Some theorists, critics, journalists and writers on the Wills would focus on his building's sculptural and formal innovations, the daring structural engineering, the cosmopolitan graphic patterns and ornament, the brave colourism, the radical playfulness, the urbane popular symbolism and the general contemporary iconicity and metropolitanism of his buildings. But, another salient aspect of Alsop's oeuvre was the multimedia/transmedia nature of his outputs, where often word, art, architecture, text and image were blurred into total, immersive spaces of ideas and ideas of spaces as much as of words, talking (rhetoric, discourse, polemic, oration) and writing (for groundbreaking websites, magazines, films and lectures) and even presenting. He was a consummate multimedia presenter of architecture – not only to paying clients but also to big TV audiences. His 2003 Channel 4 *Supercities UK* TV series in three episodes followed TV Will on a road-trip-documentary across three British 'Supercities'.[3] The application of this wholly North American invention (a coast-to-coast linear megacity was first proposed by Alan Boutwell and Mike Mitchell in 1969[4]) to the UK was original, and whilst practical, for the philistine political establishment (the ones with the money and power) it was also too risky, utopian, radical and frankly coruscating. Will's first Supercity, 'Coast to Coast' (strung around the A62 Liverpool-to-Hull motorway), was a 20-mile (32-kilometre) wide strip of 15 million inhabitants. The next three were continentalist-facing and therefore Europe-oriented concepts. These were 'Diagonale' – a 130-mile (210-kilometre) long city along the M1/M6 corridor from Birmingham to London; the once touted, but now paused, future London of the Thames Gateway project he was strongly involved in;[5] and 'Wave' – 140 miles (225 kilometres) long, from Hastings to Poole along England's South Coast. National audiences watched, for the first time, a British architect drawing their futures in ways politicians could not, and all with no more than a few coloured markers (and a bit of his genius). As an imaginative future vision for British national urban design, it has not been superseded. The *Supercity* book (2005)[6] was a 'Vision for the Future' written as a 'A prediction'[7] by Alsop.

Will Alsop, *Las Heras: An Imagined Future – Stories of an Emerging World*, 2014

Title spread of the book's first 'Story'. History and the design of the historical and historiographic, through the book and other multimedia forms, was always a concern for Alsop and the space of his designs and oeuvre.

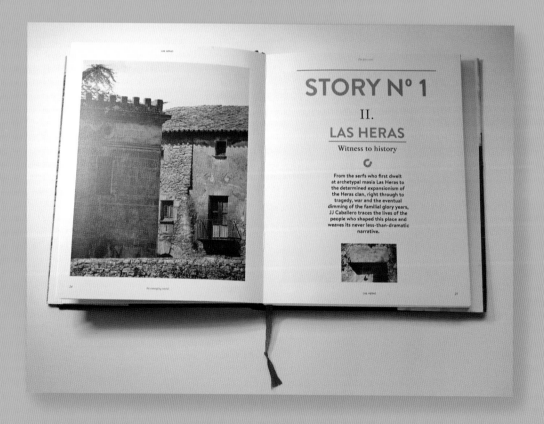

90

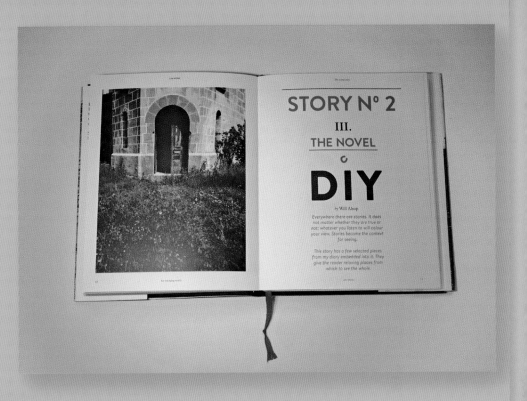

The most enigmatic of his books was Alsop's last. *Las Heras: An Imagined Future – Stories of an Emerging World* (2014) is a narratological idea of an anticipatory and proleptic space of site-specific design

The most enigmatic of his books was Alsop's last. *Las Heras: An Imagined Future – Stories of an Emerging World* (2014) is a narratological idea of an anticipatory and proleptic space of site-specific design. As he notes, it is 'a history' and a 'narrative' and is about the 'evolution' of the 'historic terrain', with 'a tangibly layered history' of Las Heras, a place of (amongst other things) 'education' and 'learning'[8] where 'there are many rooms ... all with history ... there has to be an embrace of the past along with the future'.[9] But its most beautiful treasure is snuggled comfortably within: a novel by Alsop, told by an unreliable, younger narrator (another Will) who writes things like 'I spent time thinking about design and why designers become slaves to fashion ... why don't they ever refer to the concept of cosiness?' – the Danish philosophy of *hygge*.[10]

Alsop's first published magazine article dates back to 1975 (for *NET* magazine) and was titled 'Conceptual Architecture: An Appraisal within Four Walls'.[11] The first for *AD* (1977) was 'Practice Into Theory: Speculations on Cedric Price Architects' Inter-Action Centre'.[12] From then on the range and depth of his curiosity explodes from merely the titles (which include topics as diverse as beauty, aesthetics, ecological design, the Olympics, iconic architecture, markets, the RIBA, the Royal Academy, competitions, architectural apathy, delight, John Soane and his House-Museum, time and architecture, the Thames (and Puddle Dock), conservation, preservation, Denys Lasdun, architecture by non-architects, bureaucracy, existential building, Melbourne Docklands, Peter Cook and Christine Hawley at Langen, Australia, the 21st-century art museum in London and ... his own works.

Genius Swoeuvres

Strongly blobist, podist, modulist and capsularian, design-wise at times between 1995 and 2010 he led British formal, figural and morphological digital design research, though he confessed that the computer 'sends me to sleep'.[13] Typologically he was a iconoclastic, smashing, recombining and reinventing architectural functions and programmes. After Alsop, libraries, educational buildings, public spaces, shops, museums, hotels, laboratories, offices, transport and prisons will never be the same. He believed in proportionalisms (including the golden section – 'it works'![14]) and he illustrated these with Benson & Hedges cigarette packets, tabletops, tablecloths, bars, blocks, bricks, slabs and other platonic tabula-rasas. In terms of envelopes,

skins and their tectonics, his archi-textile sensibilities transformed tensile and tensegrity structures into engineering and architectural world firsts. Technologically he was interested in the play and fun of the aesthetics of technology as much as the fun and play of technologies of aesthetics.[15] Compositionally and structurally (as his collaborating engineers will verify) he favoured and developed new forms of nonlinear and multiple cantilevers, sometimes resulting in 'stacks' of anti-gravity acrobatic architectural affects. He deployed 4th- (time) and 5th-dimensional (interaction) activation and innovations on the 5th and 6th elevations (the roofs and underneaths) of his buildings. This was a by-product of his sense of landscape and landform architecture and urbanism – the

Will Alsop's home studio,
Sheringham,
Norfolk,
2021

The space that Will once noted (in conversation) to Mark Garcia was 'most his own' and 'most his home' – the painting studio at his family home in Sheringham.

deployment of complex topologies and tectonically hyper-elaborated envelopes. These were articulated with his quintessential elevated walkways/ skybridges and piloticism. Alsop fenestration was also often deliciously riotous; one of the elevations of Peckham Library (London, 2000) is the world's first-ever completely coloured-glass façade. Zooming in, specific idea-elements, macroids, discretist pieces and other pavilion-like sibling/ child form standalone details which are distinctly Willesque and oeuvre-wide, are the iconic/ironic, pop and *objet-trouvé* symbols (some of the best parts of postmodern art) that Alsop appropriated into projects as over-scaled expressive abstractions (sometimes zoomorphic/organic/ biomorphic 'street' creatures). These

include spaceships, champagne flutes, eggs, folds, potatoes, hair, ships, pebbles, jelly beans, waves, dunes, nests, hedgehogs, dolls' houses, space invaders, teddy bears, toasters, tapestries, tights, crystals, meadows, lakes, jetties, rivers, clouds, chips, skirts, necklaces, sugar cubes, scarves, clocks, pencils, wombs, lighters, smoke and a condom.

Alsop designed and built words; sometimes lyrical, aphoristic but always aesthetic. He designed, built, spoke, exhibited, wrote, painted and sculpted these artworks, and one can delight in the panoply of these many Wills, not with nostalgia or boredom but for the more witty and joyous aesthetic and spatial futures we need now, as much as in all our futures. Δ

Notes
1. Tom Porter, *Will Alsop: The Noise*, Routledge (Abingdon), 2011, pp 156 and 159.
2. *Ibid*, p 159.
3. *Supercities UK*, written and presented by Will Alsop, directed by Simon Chu, ZCZ Films, three episodes aired in 2003 on Channel 4: www.youtube. com/watch?v=4worFDnMBSE.
4. See Alan Boutwell and Michael Mitchell, 'Planning on a National Scale', *Domus* 470, January 1969, S 6.
5. Will Alsop, 'Urbanism by the Urbaniste', in Nigel Coates (ed), *Architecture and Interiors Annual, Royal College of Art*, Royal College of Art (London), 2005.
6. Will Alsop and James Hulme, *Will Alsop's SuperCity*, Urbis (Manchester), 2005.
7. *Ibid*, p 11.
8. *Ibid*, p 9.
9. Will Alsop, *Las Heras: An Imagined Future – Stories of an Emerging World*, Rough Luxe / aLL (London), 2014, p 91.
10. *Ibid*, p 102.
11. *NET* 1975, pp 1–5.
12. Δ 47 (7–8), 1977, pp 483–6.
13. Will Alsop, 'Nothing Is Lost', lecture at the Architectural Association School of Architecture, London, 28 November 2013.
14. *Ibid*.
15. Mark Garcia, 'Playtectonics', in Coates, *op cit*.

His painting studio was the experimental laboratory where Alsop's artworks and other images, forms and spaces originated.

Kester Rattenbury

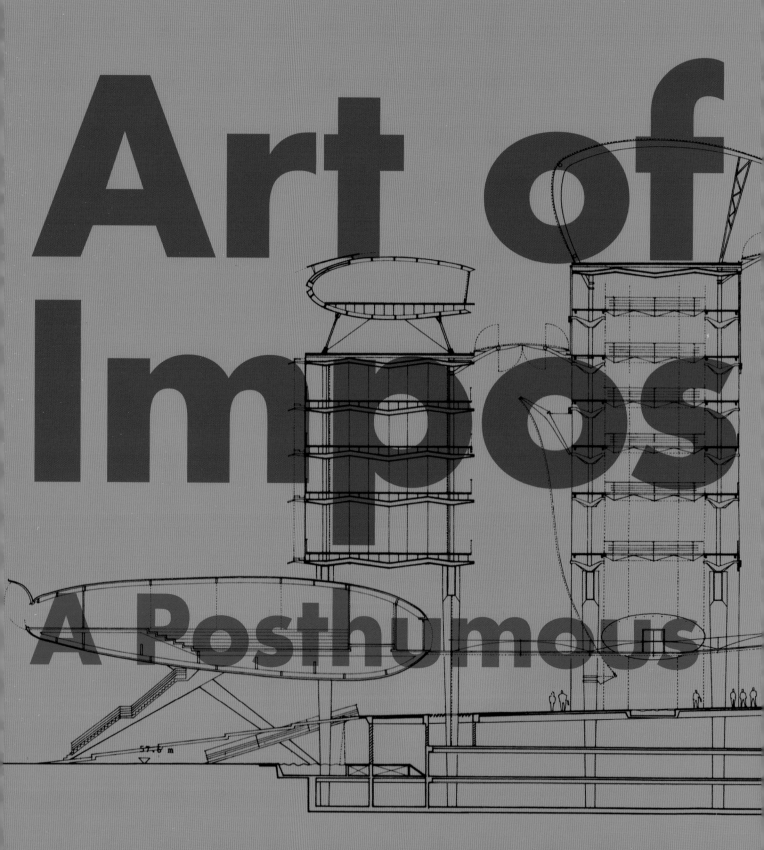

Art of
Impos
A Posthumous

57.6 m

Alsop, Lyall & Störmer,
Stage 3 section,
Hotel du Département
des Bouches-du-Rhône
('Le Grand Bleu'),
Marseille, France,
1990

The famous articulated section, showing three
administrative blocks with atria between and the
expressive 'Deliberatif' council chamber, changed
many times throughout and beyond the competition
design process and was published at all stages.
This drawing dates from the extra head-to-head
with Foster which was added after Stage 2.

the
sible

Supercrit

Kester Rattenbury convenes the long-running Supercrit series at the University of Westminster, London. Here she describes proceedings at Supercrit #8, which presented Alsop's 'Le Grand Bleu' in Marseille, France, the competition-winning building for the headquarters of the regional government of the Hôtel du Département des Bouches-du-Rhône. The event was conducted without its star performer, who had, alas, died six months prior. The invited panellists represented a range of design inputs from engineers to artists, each demonstrating their respect for Alsop and his creative verve while offering critical reflections on this ground-breaking project.

Alsop & Störmer,
Hotel du Département des Bouches-du-Rhône
('Le Grand Bleu'),
Marseille, France,
1994

'Le Grand Bleu' on completion. The Yves Klein Blue colour (incorporating façade designs by artist Brian Clarke) links the building from its gritty urban dual-carriageway location, through to the Mediterranean sea, sky and mountains.

It was always going to be impossible to hold a proper Supercrit on any project of Will Alsop's in his undeniable, far too early, absence. Supercrits are a University of Westminster research project, a live event format devised by the Experimental Practice Research Group (EXP) in the School of Architecture, that invites the world's leading architects back to school to present and debate one of their greatest projects with a panel of critics and a student audience. But the most charismatic, unexpected, challenging and rewarding of speakers, the only fully authoritative source on the unique, irreplaceable Alsop was no longer available. What on earth was the point of doing it without him?

However, there was an inescapable precedent for this event. The idea for Supercrits came from Cedric Price, Alsop's superhero, who had generously offered to help launch the fledgling research group in 2003 by presenting his Potteries Thinkbelt (1966–7) for a student audience to crit. Very sadly, Cedric died before the event took place, but the date stuck, becoming part of a weekend of celebratory events. And even in that bereft form, we found something powerful came from bringing together collaborators, friends, critics, to discuss an amazing project.

EXP came to define Supercrit projects as 'projects that changed the weather' of architectural thought and practice. The Hôtel du Département des Bouches-du-Rhône in Marseille, known as 'Le Grand Bleu' (1994), was the pivotal building of Alsop's white-knuckle, rollercoaster career, which shifted him from provocateur to someone who actually built big buildings (or rather, remarkably, did both). Yet planning the event in 2018, we found a younger generation had never heard of it. Something life-affirming about Will drove us on – caught from Alsop, perhaps (a surprising number of people at the university had worked on this project, including Camilla Wilkinson and Will McLean, who co-led the event). Just because something was impossible did not mean it should not be done.

Marseille's big blue governmental department building was certainly full of impossible things. When the competition was held in 1990, Norman Foster and Richard Rogers were only newly installed as internationally famous architects, after a decade of UK suspicion of any modern architecture at all. For a small practice like Alsop, Lyall & Störmer to make it into the final two with Foster was remarkable; to beat him was incredible. Yet Paul Finch, then editor of industry newspaper Building Design (BD), was 'absolutely certain it was going to win', as he told the Supercrit audience.

Will Alsop,
Le Grand Bleu,
Marseille, France,
1991

One of many paintings generated throughout and after project development. Supercritics emphatically argued that the paintings were not meant as direct design instructions, but shaped the ideas around the project in other ways.

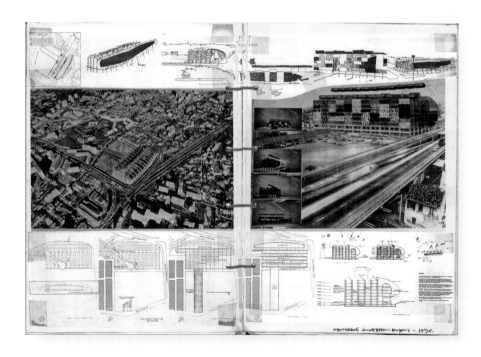

Alsop, Lyall & Störmer,
Stage 1 competition boards,
Hôtel du Département des Bouches-du-Rhône
('Le Grand Bleu'),
Marseille, France,
1990

The design was developed using original sketches by Alsop, some of them faxed from Australia, with photomontages made by Simon North using a model by Tony Reason, drawings developed by the team and panels assembled by Simon North.

This was the project where architecture and news coalesced. It was formally groundbreaking; environmentally pioneering, exploring all kinds of locally tuned and passive environmental propositions; a very early use of computer-generated design (not in the competition, but in the development); socially and politically polemical; and it was a colour – in a culture barely acclimatised to buildings being white.

Over the four years of the building's generation, *BD*'s front pages were scrapped and redesigned to follow its seismic shifts in possibility: the competition itself; the bumpy ride as the tiny practice shifted to 100+ staff; the constant, dramatic redesigns of the building forms; brief; costs. All were fed straight into *BD*. The architecture itself – the actual live design – was the news, and the profession watched as it was redesigned and remade, more or less live on the front pages of the paper, trialling democratic building forms, structural innovations, environmental and social thinking, emerging computer designs – and epically, against all odds, was actually built.

An Impossible Task

Supercrit #8 was held on 5 December 2018, in the Westminster arts venue Ambika P3. The presenters (with the impossible job of representing Alsop) were architect Jonathan Adams, who worked on the project throughout; architect and teacher Francis Graves who had joined the team; and engineer Chris McCarthy of Arup and later Battle McCarthy. Panellists were Alsop's friend and collaborator, artist and sculptor Bruce McLean, critic and friend Mel Gooding, architect-artist and teacher Sean Griffiths, Nick Johnson (Alsop's client for the New Islington project (2002–9)), Joshua Broomer of the Architecture Foundation Young Architects, and Ambika P3 founder Katharine Heron, with an audience studded with Alsop's colleagues, friends and collaborators.

Adams started by showing projects that led up to the Big Blue win: the unbuilt composite-collage tower design for Hérouville-Saint-Clair (1987–91) with Massimiliano Fuksas, Jean Nouvel and Otto Steidle (to which Will added what Fuksas called 'a big fish') and then Alsop, Lyall & Störmer's built, tiny, perforated elliptical tube for the temporary Cardiff Bay Visitor Centre (1990) and the proposal (or low-energy bubble) for the 1992 Expo in Seville (1989). All these projects set the formal scene – clearly, the next project was not going to be a 'square'. The big orange book brief for the open competition arrived by post: all in French. It nearly got thrown away, but Adams requested a translation. This was a chance to design a new democratic, expressive, local political building, on a great, gritty site on the ring road of a tough industrial Mediterranean city.

Supercrit #8,
Ambika P3,
University of Westminster,
London,
5 December 2018

Installation by Studio MASH and the Supercrit team with Eddie Blake and Gulru Arvas. The inflatable legs are half-scale models of the originals, devised and made by Camilla Wilkinson, Will McLean, Amy Chen and team. The audience are seated in a scale plan of the 'Délibératif' council chamber. Presenters, left to right: Kester Rattenbury and Will McLean (co-chairs), Chris McCarthy, Francis Graves and Jonathan Adams.

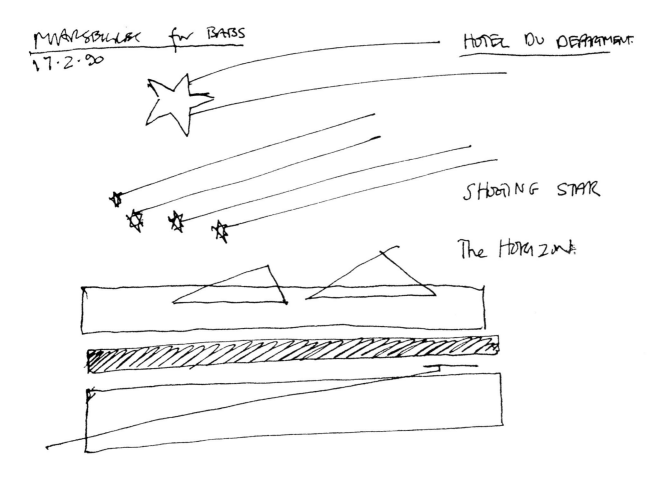

MARSEILLE for BABS
17·2·90

HOTEL DU DEPARTMENT.

SHOOTING STAR

The Horizont

Will Alsop,
First sketch,
'Le Grand Bleu',
Marseille, France,
1990

The first sketch, in Alsop's notebook, was one of those faxed back to the Alsop & Lyall office from Australia. The design process began in a largely pre-digital design world, though the project would become one of the first to showcase 3D computer design. The sketch already shows a project seeking to embrace the climate and location, and fusing the imagined design with sky, sea and horizon.

Will's sketches – faxed back to his office from a trip to Australia in a pre-digital world – started to emerge: stars, sea, sky; a building of parts, elevated on legs, curved like Seville, perforated like Cardiff, demonstrably opening up to the public. Dirigibles and other ideas which Alsop linked with Cedric Price appeared: movement, bridges, gantries – a building activated by people. To everyone's surprise, Adams recalled, a 'very conceptual' model, collaged onto the site photos, and 'really rough' competition panels pushed Alsop & Störmer (as the practice was now called) through to the second stage.

As in the competition for Paris's Centre Pompidou (1971), in which a very young Alsop and team was runner-up, Arup was brought in, conferring the promise of do-ability. They immediately took up the structural issues and the passive strategies for the intense summer heat and high winds of Marseille, introducing acoustic considerations (a noisy, roadside site) and 3D computer work. The emerging composition of administration buildings and 'Déliberatif' (the expressive council chamber designed to make debate public, visible and permanent) kept morphing: elements grew, shrank, briefly became more 'white and more considered' at second stage (the paintings Will produced throughout the design were not at first predominantly blue, but animated, animal-ish) and moved on.

Those drawings could be time-lapsed to animate and show the evolving design process: at one point the office atria opened, roofed by a balloon structure which could be raised and lowered (à la Seville). At another there was a rooftop greenhouse where workers could pick tomatoes for their lunch. By the time Adams had finished his laborious detailed drawings, they had all been superseded.

Chris McCarthy took on the story. He had been drafted in from Arup, a maverick engineer in his own right. 'Alsop was my Mozart – I still hum his work ... he liberated people.' Alsop agreed to take him on, 'as long as you don't make anything I like', McCarthy recalled. Arup had lost money on Pompidou, but nonetheless backed the Marseille project to the hilt (they had been competition engineers for both Foster and Alsop teams). For Will, constraints became opportunities. McCarthy described him saying, '"Yes, it's bloody windy. We'll use the wind to shape the building ... The Mistral wind comes over the building, drives the ventilation. Easy!" ... Will was the engineer, artist, accountant ... everything.'

Foster was inevitably expected to win. At second stage, Foster arrived in his own helicopter; the Alsop team by cheap flight and old van; their model – dropped and broken by annoyed taxi drivers – was fixed late at night with glue and a bottle of whisky ('It looks better!' Alsop had said). When pushed to an extra third stage, against the unbeatable Foster, Alsop responded by getting the easel out, and setting his paintings in front of the Foster display boards. McCarthy recounted Massimiliano Fuksas, a member of the jury, saying that 'Foster's building was brilliant ... it could be built anywhere.' But the Alsop & Störmer scheme related to wind, sun, colours, people. 'It could only be built in Marseille.' They had won.

Another Kind of Thinking
Francis Graves – then a young, French-speaking British architect working in Marseille – continued the Supercrit with an account of the meeting when the clients discussed whether the whole exterior was going to be blue – an inconceivable discussion in 1990s Britain. For Will, any problem was a design opportunity. When told to cut £1 million off the project, Will said: 'Great. We can redesign it.' He was a 'design junkie', said Graves, describing how the switch from 10.8-metre (35-foot) structural grid (between office and parking levels) to 5.4-metre (17.5-foot) office grid generated the

Supercrit #8,
Ambika P3,
University of Westminster,
London,
5 December 2018

Chris McCarthy presenting, with chairs Kester Rattenbury and Will McLean and co-panellist Francis Graves. The ever-changing series of sectional drawings can be seen in the background.

'brilliant' crossed columns; how the Délibératif building's aerofoil shape was designed (in paper models) so as to be all clad in flat identical triangular panels; and so on.

Graves ended where the discussion started, on Alsop's paintings. When panellist Sean Griffiths suggested the building was not enough like them, co-panellists weighed in. 'I don't want the buildings to look like the paintings,' said Bruce McLean. 'No,' agreed Mel Gooding, continuing: 'They are expressive of another kind of thinking ... trying to get rid of any thinking at all.' McLean had tutored Alsop to ditch his ideas before painting: 'we were pretty fierce with him' (although, Gooding added, Alsop was brilliant at 'subtly stealing' ideas from others). Nor were the paintings used schematically by the office, said Adams. They shaped the project in other ways – like one entirely unconnected with the building form, which established something big and blue.

Alsop conceived an exuberant, proudly regional, polemically open building – a place where the public could observe elected representatives doing their job, and where janitor and Président would share a cafe table. So, amongst other things, this project was the great exemplar of the struggle of architecture through procurement: 'the corruption of process' as Nick Johnson expressed it.

On winning the project, the office expanded again from about 15 to 100+, many staff coming from the very practices Alsop was trying to challenge – inevitably bringing a more mainstream high-tech way of doing things. That, Adams explained 'couldn't be held back ... especially as much work was now being done with computers'. But 'Marseille was the one building where I felt creative on site', Graves said. The office determinedly worked with a local project manager – and 36 specialist contractors who would all 'line up on site' wanting to contribute, successfully, to the process.

Architectural writer and historian Jeremy Melvin steered the discussion back to the great political ambitions and struggles of this building. 'It was a project,' Nick Johnson suggested, 'which had to stand up to being corrupted.' Adams especially regretted the loss of the big, open, democratic space under the administrative block (taken over by incorporating more offices): 'At the time I felt it's not the project that we designed ... we had to make the best of it.' The loss of the more open, perforated façade meant Alsop was able to bring in glass artist Brian Clarke, but 'the great emblematic polemic offer of public space', said Johnson, '[is] now entirely emblematic'. Gooding was 'appalled to hear the building is no longer easy to access … this space gives ownership of the city to the people, and it would be a tragedy if that were lost.'

A Spirit of Optimism

'So, in what ways has the weather been changed?' Katharine Heron asked, prompting an avalanche of responses. The spectacular boom–bust cycles of Alsop's subsequent career path ('of which his family', McCarthy said, 'were the real heroes') – and in which no idea was too big to be tackled in real practice – were launched by this project. The way his design processes (so immediately shared through *BD*) fed straight into other people's design thinking – 'long before social media', said Adams. Form, environmental invention, colour, generosity, joy, were raised by many, while Heron also suggested that to 'master the financial decision-making processes in the making of a local authority building is quite unique'. Using conceptual processes 'right through to conception on site' added Graves. 'Paintings which are not the designs – the extraordinary delivery of a very complicated building … The spirit of optimism,' Heron added. 'Proof that you could do it,' said Adams.

And the building? 'It's the single most brilliant realisation of a particular notion of political architecture – the philosophy implicit in building … a completely perfect … visual, sculptural, conceptual … demonstration of what its purpose is,' said Gooding. 'Will's clearly best building' (developer Roger Zogolovitch). And 'the last moment of the age of innocence … when a practice of five could enter such a project – and win it', said Johnson, adding that the 600 pages of risk assessment required today 'has not meant we're building better buildings'.

Following a discussion on how you cannot photograph a good painting, Bruce McLean helped to conclude, 'When I saw that building I could not believe how good it is. That building is unphotographable. Thank God something is.' Reviewing it for *BD* in 1994 was indeed a delight: a big, blue, wonderful building-creature which transfigures that unlovely part of the city, with all the dramatic, articulated ambiguities of its political spaces tied straight through, with its Yves Klein Blue magic, to the Mediterranean mountains, sea and sky. A place one does not want to leave. ∆

Studio MASH / Gil_design, Supercrit #8 poster, 2018

The poster was designed by Studio MASH with Gil_design, a young graphic design firm with its own roots in Marseille. Studio MASH managed and curated design of the Supercrit installation with Kester Rattenbury and the team. Supercrit #8 can be seen at www.supercrits.com/8/.

BUILD KNOW

Describing the making and thinking behind a film shot at Alsop & Störmer's Stirling Prize-winning Peckham Library, **Thomas Aquilina** portrays how the building and its public piazza has democratised a previously neglected patch of South London, providing not just reading materials but much needed community functions for a diverse part of the capital. Much of the building's formal dexterity happens above its users' heads, deploying the familiar Alsop trope of touching the ground lightly.

INGLEDGE

REFLECTIONS ON PECKHAM LIBRARY

Peckham Library is a site of intersection and aspiration. This radical building was a hopeful symbol of the new millennium and remains a place to nurture the futures of its diverse local community. It is a building to consider both the architect as conductor of a collaborative design process and an architectural form characterised by openness.

Designed by Alsop & Störmer, Peckham Library opened to the public in 2000, gaining the Stirling Prize that same year. A response to an ambitious brief set by Southwark Council, the 2,300 square metre (24,750 square foot) project is a dominant but intimate building. Architect Will Alsop wanted to reinvent the static public library of Victorian philanthropists and demystify the typology with his design for Peckham Library by inspiring curiosity in the South London neighbourhood.

The film *Peckham Library: Afterparti in Conversation with Christophe Egret, Hanif Kara & Tszwai So* (2022)[1] was produced for the Architecture Foundation's year-long film series 'AF Turns 30', which reflected on London landmarks built in the last 30 years. As part of Afterparti's wider exploration into contemporary urban space through the lenses of identity and race, the profiling of the library illustrates how co-existing identities interact. For example, it reflects the needs of the local community in creating spaces for musicality and poetry, while drawing on diaspora heritage through symbolic registers found in African and Caribbean countries. The making of Peckham Library and what it continues to represent today marks a hybrid architecture that blends influences from near and afar.

An Architecture of Generosity

The sensory hints of migration along the lively street of Rye Lane are tangible as one approaches the library, passing by subdivided shop interiors, heading north towards Peckham Square. Drawing closer, the word 'LIBRARY' – in huge, metallic capital letters – comes into view, perched atop the building. The large lettering is reminiscent of the Victorian era when signage was considered an artform used to signify services offered. The square where Peckham Library sits is at the end of Rye Lane, framed by Peckham Arch – a tensile fabric and steel structure designed by Troughton McAslan in 1994. Moving through the arch, the square opens up to an undefined space with two public buildings flanking each side: Peckham Pulse Leisure Centre and the library.

On arriving at the building's edge, the library's civic presence has a surprisingly diminutive footprint. The vivid colour palette, copper exterior, bold lettering, leaning columns and textured surfaces combine to make it stand out, its iconic form resembling an inverted 'L' shape that cantilevers 12 metres (around 40 feet) above ground to create a covered plaza. Peckham Library choreographs urban life around it. People crisscross the square to arrive at the plaza, bringing them to the front door of the library. They are drawn into the library, or to pass beneath it. The plaza encourages them to cycle,

Afterparti,
Stills from *Peckham Library: Afterparti in Conversation with Christophe Egret, Hanif Kara & Tszwai So,* 2022

left: The approach to Peckham Square, framed by Peckham Arch, with Peckham Library's south-facing façade in view. The roof's protruding orange 'beret' acts as a shade for a study centre on the top floor.

below left: The library plaza as formed by the two-storey reading room cantilever with a steel mesh reinforcing the external edges. The plaza is open on three sides, enlarging the space for pedestrian access.

below right: Side elevation showing the pre-patinated green copper exterior finish. The cantilevered block is supported by steel columns rising from ground level, and was developed using a prototype BIM system.

The making of Peckham Library and what it continues to represent today marks a hybrid architecture that blends influences from near and afar

watch, listen, linger, host markets, play table tennis or even join a dance parade. Although the plaza is dark, even in the middle of the day, people continue to congregate there. It is a space of multiple happenings and invites a rich informality.

In the film, the library's structural engineer, Hanif Kara of AKT II, stands outside the main entrance, waiting to show us around. He wears an orange top that matches the colour of the library roof's 'beret'. His excitement at returning to this building, a pivotal project in his career, is palpable. He explains that the plaza's most important feature is its seven angled columns, which appear to be placed at random along the length of the cantilever. The playful arrangement of these slender circular columns was imagined by Alsop as a haven for skateboarders. The landscaping around the columns provides a place for people to skate on, around, over and through. Kara describes the group of columns as 'the legs of a giraffe', and using a pen to air-sketch the compound geometry explains that the columns have a pivot point and can move around within that. Though they may appear irregularly positioned, they were in fact parametrically modelled.

We enter the building and take the lift to the fourth floor. Bypassing the administrative spaces at the library's lower levels, we move directly up to the public area and book stacks. When the building was first completed, the north-facing glazed façade provided a panoramic view of the city as you ascended in the lift. This view was obstructed in 2018 by the comparatively sober elevations of Mountview Academy of Theatre Arts designed by Carl Turner Architects.

Upon exiting the lift and entering the main reading room, we encounter a long horizontal volume broken up by three pods that are also elevated on stilts. The dancing columns from the plaza protrude through the floor into this space. The outside comes in through a long narrow window facing Rye Lane, revealing a sliver of the shopping arcades. The pods, sitting above the heads of the library's visitors, were based on African pots and provide study spaces and meeting rooms. These capsules are clad with timber panels stapled together. The impossibility of drawing these panels in the design phase meant they had to be improvised directly on site. Kara shares an anecdote about Alsop, who suggested taking advantage of Mad Cow Disease, prevalent at the time of the build, by encasing the pods in free surplus leather. As Kara so puts it in the film, Alsop was 'part architect, part artist and part philosopher'.

Alsop and the services engineer Battle McCarthy sought out natural methods of ventilating the building. In addition to the concrete frame of the main block, the density of books is utilised to naturally cool the space, which was a new method at the time. Our walk pauses in the elevated reading room, attempting to find what remains of the previously impressive view of the city. Kara shares his sentiments on the project, feeling vindicated that this building has been embraced by the local community. It has taught him that as a designer, people do not need to see him as 'an Indian guy from Africa, but simply as someone with the potential to change places'.

The main reading room looking southwards with one of three stilted timber-framed pods. The pod structures were designed to resemble African pots and constructed using curved timber ribs with structural plywood inner and outer skins.

The section on Black Writing in the main reading room. Latest statistics from Southwark Council (2017) indicate that Peckham, with a population of 15,010, has a total BAME population of 71 per cent, making it one of the UK's most diverse neighbourhoods.

The panel conversation hosted by Thomas Aquilina and Siufan Adey of Afterparti with Christophe Egret, Hanif Kara and Tszwai So at the White Collar Factory in London. The conversation explored Peckham Library's past, present and future, revealing issues of power, community and ownership.

The Architect as Conductor

From a walk to a dialogue, understanding Peckham Library is as much about outside perspective as it is about lived experience. The library as a typology is a form of social infrastructure where people can articulate their needs and access resources to realise their aspirations. A library is a distinctive public habitat. Their value as a physical space fixed in an urban context is enhanced by their contents being able to transpose visitors to imaginary places. Peckham Library has to embrace the predominantly Black population, their histories rooted in Africa and the Caribbean, and the needs of migrants who reshape and expand their claim on an area. A reflection of this history is seen in the library's showcasing a bronze bust of Harold Moody – a Jamaican-born doctor who made Peckham his home and founded the League of Coloured Peoples in 1931.

The historical context of the library is further explored in the film through a panel conversation at the White Collar Factory in London with Kara, Christophe Egret (the project architect of Peckham Library who would go on to establish his own practice, Studio Egret West, in 2004) and Tszwai So of Spheron Architects who is currently working on the redesign of Peckham Square. During the discussion, we retrospectively assess the development of the library, the current reimagining of the square and the future of community spaces. The temporal shifting of a space such as a library shows how an architect, and their team, can act as conductors in the past, present and future contexts.

The building was designed during the peak of the New Labour government in the UK: a time of optimism and risk-taking. Fred Manson, former Director of Regeneration at Southwark Council, was interested in commissioning an iconic piece of architecture as part of the council-led regeneration plan. During his tenure, he gained recognition for delivering the Millennium Bridge and transformed a power station into Tate Modern in 2000. Similarly, Egret describes the Peckham Library project as 'an architecture with presence', although presence is not necessarily monumental. He speaks of a technique Alsop had adopted 'to make buildings touch the ground gently'. The softness was intended to inspire young people to engage with the library. Kara points out, 'if you could get an eight-year-old in the building, it was likely they would return to the library for the rest of their lives'.

A reading of Peckham Library in its context coupled with the conversations captured in the making of the film reveal how the forming of a library is principally about building knowledge for a local community

The children's play space with expressed concrete cross-bracing and multicoloured north-facing structural glazing. In exposing the structure, the function of the interior spaces are made visible externally.

Critical to the library's success with locals was community consultation, incorporating multiple voices early in the design process, sometimes using drawing and painting to discuss ideas. The role of the library was not tethered solely to books, but as the plan was refined through consultation, a relationship to music and poetry grew with it, alongside a dedicated area for children and a desire to possess a view of the city. This kind of engagement ensured the building programmed an Afro-Caribbean space, and in turn the three pods on the fourth floor each became spaces responding directly to the community. In this way, architects can perform like conductors who catalyse ideas into particular trajectories.

Looking towards the future, Spheron Architects have embarked on the redesign of Peckham Square. Wanting to be rooted in the area, So has relocated his architectural office to the high street in Peckham. As the first legacy project under the Southwark Stands Together Initiative,[2] a response to the Black Lives Matter movement, the project is committed to public engagement and understanding the lived experience of the community. So remarks: 'This initiative is to reach out to the silent, underrepresented majority of Peckham.' While the designs of the square are still being formed, it appears it will respond directly to the qualities of Peckham Library. For the square to be successful in its transformation it will need to engender a sense of local habitation, encourage circulation and maintain a conversation with the performative nature of the library building.

Enduring Legacy
A reading of Peckham Library in its context coupled with the conversations captured in the making of the film reveal how the forming of a library is principally about building knowledge for a local community. Peckham Library inspired a new generation of designs for libraries that attempted to suture themselves into the social and urban fabric, such as the Idea Stores in Tower Hamlets, East London, by Adjaye Associates, completed in 2004 and 2005. Peckham Library remains architecturally relevant today and serves to remind emerging designers and architects that imbuing playfulness and aspiration can empower residents. It is an examplar of how making a building out of local knowledge ensures its survival. ∆

Notes
1. Afterparti, *Peckham Library: Afterparti in Conversation with Christophe Egret, Hanif Kara & Tszwai So* (Architecture Foundation, 2022): www.youtube.com/watch?v=QeW9luZNZUM.
2. Southwark Public Health Division, 'Southwark Stands Together: Findings from Listening Events, Roundtables and an Online Survey', London, May 2021: https://consultations.southwark.gov.uk/housing-community-services-department-community-engagement-team/southwark-stands-together/results/sstresultsandrecommendations.pdf.

aLL Design,
Painting in the
Vyner Street studio,
East London,
2019

A project painting developed by team members Marcos
Rosello, Maxine Pringle and Tom Bower for the design
development of a mixed-use residential project in Portslade
on England's south coast. The painting looked at evolving the
concept with references to the industrial history of the location.

Marcos Rosello

Back to His Roots

aLL Design – the Legacy of an All-inclusive Architect

Alsop's last incarnation of architectural practice, aLL Design was co-founded with **Marcos Rosello** in 2011. Rosello recounts Alsop's tirelessly hospitable open-door policy in the studio, which promoted an atmosphere of benevolent multidisciplinary design exploration. The guiding principles the practice carries forward by way of legacy were set out during this period.

When aLL Design was established in 2011, the team knew it would be Will's last studio. We decided it would be entirely under his design control, which is when he was happiest and at his most productive. His core value of wanting 'to make life better' was fundamental to our ethos and was understood to be intrinsic to any future iterations of the practice. While discussing what to call the studio, Will was clear that he did not want his name to be in the company name. That way, the studio would be in a strong position to carry on this ethos after he retired and no longer had direct design input. And that is how the name aLL Design came about – reflecting an all-encompassing ethos for designing anything, for all: from a teaspoon to a city.

The Garden

Will inhabited the office much like a home; the door at the premises in Vyner Street, East London (which we moved to in 2015) was always open, and we punched a hole through one wall and created the garden. Memorable moments, where the team would see him in his element, were when students popped by to visit. They wanted to learn from one of the best creative-thinker-architects of his generation. Invariably, he would let them stay for hours, chatting about projects in the studio or out in garden.

Will made sure he was universally accessible to everyone. He loved to talk and share knowledge through his projects, articles and teachings, and he held professorships at several universities in the UK and

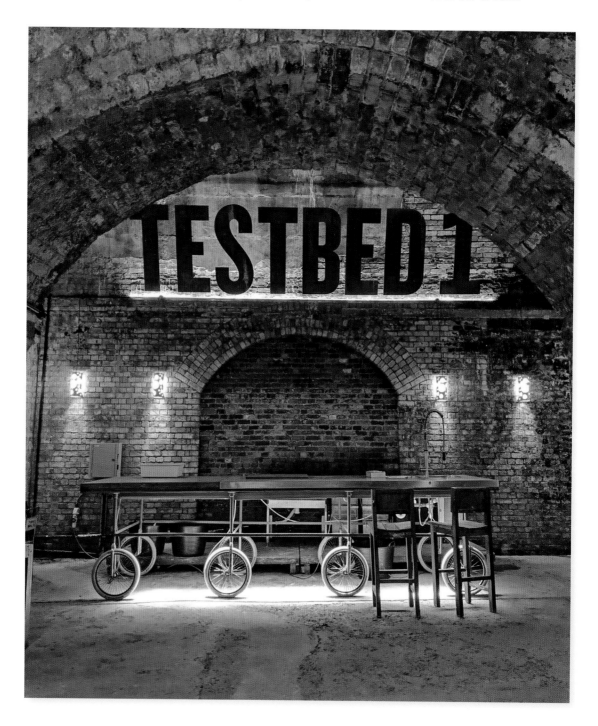

aLL Design,
Testbed1,
London Bridge,
London,
2016

The first Testbed was in a large warehouse complex in Parkgate Road, Battersea, used for workshops, exhibitions and events curated by Will Alsop and friends. It moved with Doodle Bar beneath railway arches in Druid Street, London Bridge, in 2016 when the original site was sold for redevelopment.

aLL Design,
SuperCity model for Manchester,
Vyner Street studio,
East London,
2016

Sketch model made for an exhibition of the
SuperCity project in 2004, with Will Alsop in
the background. SuperCity was Will's vision
of how the future of the north of England
could be, from coast to coast along the M62,
incorporating transport, living, commuting
and sustainable design.

abroad. Throughout his career and all his partnerships and
ventures, he spent a huge amount of time talking, writing,
drawing, designing and debating with people about art,
architecture and design. aLL Design endeavours to continue
this tradition, merging teaching and practice through
associations at Cambridge and Portsmouth universities in
the UK, YACademy in lecturing and design competitions in
Italy and, more recently, at Doha University in Qatar.

The office was not just an architectural studio; it was a
place of education, exploration and fun that would often
carry on after work. Often, it would spill out to the Doodle
Bar, an event space Will set up with Squint/Opera and friend
Kevin Cassandro, first in Battersea then as part of Testbed1
in London Bridge. The office felt more like a place of learning
than just a place of work, and Will wanted to be sure this
was incorporated into the studio's DNA. One way he did
this was to hire new talent fresh out of university – people
who could bring new ideas and new ways of presenting.
He believed them to be the most open to ideas, adding new
perspectives to the ever-evolving debate.

aLL Design
'Street Creature',
Doha, Qatar,
2021

Rather than designing a traditional dual-aspect advertising structure, the project followed the studio's 'street creature' philosophy by creating a more sculptural proposal with a 360-degree panoramic advertising ribbon, integrated water supply and seating – a place where people can not only get information but some shade, water and a bit of 'you time'.

Will's design process included different people from the aLL Design team from concept to completion. We try to emulate this today. We start with a literal blank canvas, a large, floor-to-ceiling stretched canvas ready for painting. Working alongside initial sketch ideas, we use the canvas to make collaborative, layered paintings that help free the designers' minds from preconceptions of what a response to a brief should be, and to record aspirations of what the project could be. The drawings and images are developed at design reviews where the whole office offers input. This method invites everyone to take a major role in developing ideas. Where Will carefully guided this process, we now encourage different team members to lead because it helps them grow and take ownership of their ideas. It is very important to aLL Design that the team continually develops their creativity and skills to become more complete designers, rather than doing the same repetitive work again and again.

Rose-Tinted Glasses

Will always looked on the bright side of things. Whether it was project-related or personal, he saw the positives and never understood why people would be negative. He trusted what people said, and did not mind if people did not like his work, although he preferred it if they did. And if the work did not prompt an emotional response, he considered he had failed. This outlook could and did get him into difficulties personally and in business, but as a creative driver, it made the architecture.

One of his preferred ways to manage a studio was to partner with other practices. Early on we adopted this strategy for international projects, and it worked very well. Learning from Will's previous partnership experiences – some more successful than others – we make sure we are working with a people-orientated practice. We have since found an enduring synergy with Corstorphine & Wright, who empower our approach by giving us the backing of a skilled delivery team.

aLL Design and Corstorphine & Wright,
Headquarters building,
Surrey, England,
2021

A joint submission, the design focused on creating a central space that would encourage people to meet and discuss. The team created a variety of so-called 'bump pods' – seating areas for impromptu conversations.

aLL Design,
Testbed2,
Chongqing, China,
2021

The China Testbed, on a former money factory, demonstrates the studio's 'knock nothing down' principle. The masterplan activates in-between spaces and includes sites for key interventions by other designers to infill over time. Testbed2 is now an exemplar of regeneration and a popular tourist destination.

aLL Design,
Cheesecake,
Chongqing, China,
2018

Included in the studio's 'street creatures' category, the Cheesecake building is sculptural architecture with a function. A meanwhile space, part of the first phase of the regeneration of a large steel mill, it is a kiosk that can be used for multiple events to promote understanding and awareness of the future of the site.

aLL Design,
Boutique Hotel and Beach Club,
Doha, Qatar,
2021

below: Initial concept design sketch for a proposal by aLL Design office member Ned Drury, showing an elevated boutique hotel, glamping pods with a beach club, food outlets and a club restaurant, with a circular promenade that forms a ring around the site.

right: Digital visualisation showing an aerial view of the hotel and beach club.

aLL Design's office in Chongqing, China, 2016

Will Alsop (right) and office member George Wade (left) sleep off jetlag before the opening of an exhibition in the China studio.

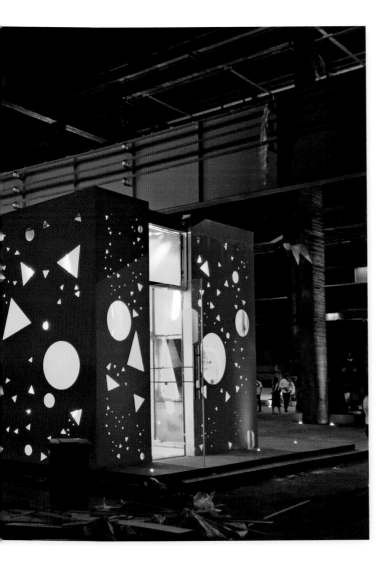

Once everything settled down after Will's passing, aLL Design team members old and new reflected on and celebrated his life. We discussed how to move forward, and this prompted a conversation not so much about how to pursue a style, but about how to continue a design ethos. Today we describe the central tenets of our practice as: 'make life better' – for people and places by highlighting individual identity; 'knock nothing down' – demolition is not an option unless a building is dangerous, because memories and a sense of place enhance an existing grain; 'testBed' – an interest in meanwhile spaces, community engagement and collaboration; and 'street creatures' – site-specific sculptural architectures with a function.

All in all, Will had a great impact on us in the office, and on the consultants and clients he worked with. Our tenets are just a guide and it will be enjoyable to see how past and present staff develop their own ideas and how the practice evolves in the future. There is no doubt though, we all miss Will very much. ⌀

A Word from
Δ∇ Editor
Neil Spiller

Five Cigaret or Seven?

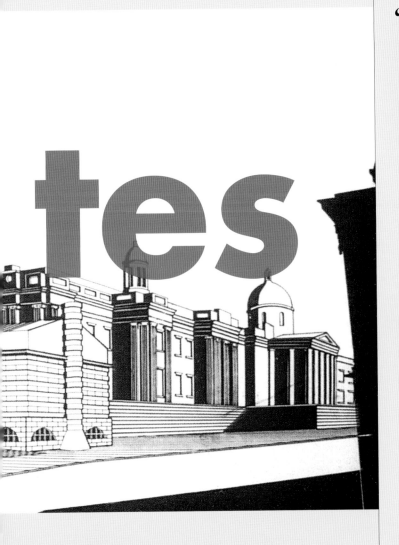

'ARCHITECTURE is a compounded historical development. This historical process is the grounds for art as a sophisticated cultural discipline. The ARCHITECTURE of Civilisation.'

— Will Alsop, 1996[1]

It is the height of summer in 1985 and I am sitting with Will Alsop in a pub, the Cooper's Arms, at the end of Flood Street, close to the King's Road in London.

I had grown a full beard, one of only two I have cultivated in my whole adulthood. It was hot and my beard made me sweat: I had underestimated how far down the King's Road access to Flood Street was and had rushed there, carrying my heavy A1 portfolio under my aching arm, fearing I would be late. When I got to the office of Alsop & Lyall, situated in the old Flood Street power station, and after trudging up the stairs, I found the office door locked and no-one responding to my more and more anxious knocks. My appointment was for noon; by 12:45, I was about to leave with a heavy sense of disappointment when I heard other trudging footsteps coming up the stairs. It was Alsop, a roll of dyelines under his arm. He apologised for being late (apparently a client meeting that had overrun). He muttered an expletive on finding no-one in the office, said he knew what pub they would be in, and ushered me down the stairs into the street and to the Cooper's Arms – but to his dismay they were not in there either. We had a chat and a couple of drinks and then returned to the office: its friendly and not numerous population had returned from its lunchtime shenanigans. So what passed as a very informal interview for a post-Masters year-out job began.

What had got me into this position had been a series of fortunate events that started when one of my tutors at Thames Polytechnic School of Architecture asked our group what architects they should invite for our school's open lecture series. I immediately said 'Will Alsop'. I had known the practice's monochrome drawing work since the previous year, had seen the iconic '40 under 40' exhibition at the Royal Institute of British Architects (RIBA) at which they had been represented, and had also been studying the amazingly evocative eruptions of colour and more free-flowing Hamburg City Centre paintings (1984–5) that had recently been published.

Alsop & Lyall,
Riverside Studios,
Hammersmith, London,
1982

The Riverside Studios proposal was compositionally defined by the contrast between the rather Florentine, extruded forms with punched-in square windows and stripy roof planes and the more standalone pavilions.

**Alsop & Lyall,
Hamburg City Centre,
Germany,
1984–5**

These paintings for an unbuilt project,
and others like them, were the first
time Neil Spiller had seen Alsop's
flamboyant yet quickly honed and
suggestive representations – projecting an
architectural world of colourful fun.

So a few weeks later, I was sitting in a lecture hall;
Will Alsop was at the lectern and immediately enquired
of his hosts, 'Have you booked me for a five-cigarette
talk or a seven-cigarette talk?' Seven, they replied
jokingly. He gave a wonderful, insightful and witty
talk, fully exposing his iconoclastic personality, and as
he extinguished the butt of his seventh cigarette, he
stopped mid-sentence and asked where the toilet was.
In a fit of uncharacteristic pushing myself forward, I
waited for him to emerge from his ablutions and asked
him what I should do to apply for a job. 'Send me some
pictures' was all he said. During the 'interview', he
explained it was the photographs of my drawings that
had interested him and he was not worried about my
woeful office experience to date.

121

He examined the drawings I had brought with me and I launched into the influences and narrative that had made me compose both the architecture and the way I had represented it on the drawings. He then, kindly but a little irritated, said: 'Look, it doesn't matter what you have to tell yourself to make work of this quality and originality, it could be stories about Noddy and Big Ears [it was actually about John Ruskin's *Seven Lamps of Architecture*], but you don't need to bore me with it, the project is enough.'

The Hamburg project was of considerable size and should it progress they would need more staff. He said ring in a couple of weeks and maybe it will have been given the green light. I almost skipped down the King's Road to the tube station, thinking soon I'd be working for two of my heroes on a glamorous international project. But, alas, it was not to be: after calling every two weeks for the next two months, it became clear that Hamburg was not going to happen.

Charisma and Birmingham

Alsop was a charismatic and generous, benevolent teacher as well as a maverick architect. In the early 1990s I was partially involved with what is now called Birmingham City University, then situated in the Perry Barr area of the city. Phil Watson, my soon-to-be teaching partner at the Bartlett School of Architecture, University College London (UCL), was running the Diploma course there. Alsop was a friend to the course, offering drawing board space at his office to students who wanted to have a work base in London, and the members of the office would help crit the work. Alsop's insight on these projects was, of course, highly regarded and many students benefited from this simple generosity. I was lucky enough to be on some of these sessions. Alsop also employed some of my graduating students from the Bartlett, as well as other Bartlett alumni, nurturing them, giving them an experience unachievable anywhere else and a burgeoning self-confidence. Many have flowered into well-known and respected architects in their own right. Staff and students could immediately sense Alsop's love of art and architecture and his synthesis of the two. He had little respect for received wisdom or the fetishisation of architectural detail. I remember a short tirade against the Hi-Tech architects and their obsession with the grommet, at a lecture given at the RIBA in the late 1980s.

Neil Spiller,
Truth Atrium – Floral Hall Site,
Covent Garden,
Diploma thesis,
Architectural Association (AA)
School of Architecture, London,
1985

One of the drawings Neil Spiller showed Will Alsop on the day of the Flood Street interview. This particular drawing explores the interior space of the Truth Atrium, one of seven around which Spiller's thesis project, a new School of Architecture for the AA, was designed.

Alsop was a charismatic and generous, benevolent teacher as well as a maverick architect

There were many lectures, crits, drinks, dinners and most importantly conversations between us over the years. I specifically remember one convened at the Barbican in London to coincide with the 'Future City' exhibition in 2006, which I chaired, between Nigel Coates and Alsop: a very enjoyable and light-hearted chat which ranged from the catalytic notion of the city, infrastructure and the personal agency of architects to issues of style and fun. I could feel the large audience drinking up every sentence.

Freedom at Point Zero

When, in 2010, I decided to leave the Bartlett and reinvigorate the tired University of Greenwich's School of Architecture and Construction, Alsop was one of the first I called on for thoughts and help. To this, as usual, he responded enthusiastically, coming down to the campus at Avery Hill in Eltham, Southeast London, a place he had no idea where he was, to do a lecture. Dinner, drinks and joviality followed. Shortly after that our new building in central Greenwich was built and Alsop again returned to lecture, this time in state-of-the-art facilities and a much easier place to get to.

For many years the epicentre of Alsopian activity seemed to reside in London's Battersea. He wanted his business partners to gain experience as teachers and again wanted his office to nurture students and help them thrive. He invited me and a colleague to this part of town to the 'Doodle Bar' to discuss us giving a unit to the practice. All discussions were conducted on the 'beach' – a rather ramshackle exterior space overlooking a small, fetid dock, where someone had dumped a pile of sand. Some pints and a bottle of red wine later and the deal was done.

Alsop liked the idea of making spaces that were dependent on the vitality of mixing scales of use, of ad hoc social interaction, sometimes choreographed and sometimes not, and a growing sense of community where work and play were not separated and fun was everywhere. His idea of the 'Doodle Bar' was all this and more.

In recognition of Alsop's generosity towards myself and other generations of students and young architects, I recommended him for an Honorary Doctorate. The award was accepted happily by Alsop; it was by no means his first such award and one might say he was already highly decorated. It was bestowed in the beautiful Chapel that is part of the centre of the Old Royal Naval College in Greenwich, amongst the architecture of Wren, Hawksmoor and Vanbrugh – a more appropriate place I cannot think of! With characteristic gusto Alsop beguiled the graduating students with his calm voice and inspirational words about creativity, being true to oneself and never letting anything stand in one's way.

After the ceremony – which always conspires to be on a hot July day, when being dressed in black robes

**Alsop & Lyall,
Hamburg City Centre, Germany,
1984–5**

The project still shows a preoccupation with the stripe, pseudo-rusticating extruded façades with square punched-in windows and openings that this time are combined with non-orthogonal forms and a metallic exoskeleton. This project and Riverside Studios are certainly architectural siblings.

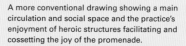

A more conventional drawing showing a main circulation and social space and the practice's enjoyment of heroic structures facilitating and cossetting the joy of the promenade.

Alsop liked the idea of making spaces that were dependent on the vitality of mixing scales of use, of ad hoc social interaction, sometimes choreographed and sometimes not, and a growing sense of community where work and play were not separated and fun was everywhere

and a mortarboard in the dense sunlight can make participants a tad grumpy – many students wanted to photograph Alsop, who obliged without rancour, even though he was hungry and no doubt thirsty. At lunch in the dining room reputed to have been Captain Cook's (whether this is true or not, I am unsure), Alsop and I tried to sell the university an Alsop painting – to no avail, but it provided an intermission of hilarity in what can be stifling and boring events. With Alsop there, the world seemed brighter.

This I think was the last time I saw him. I did not know when I shook his hand, patted him on the arm and bade him farewell that it would be forever. I hope this Δ ignites interest in Alsop for those who do not know of him (you should do), and further excites those who do. Δ

Notes
1. Will Alsop, 'The Context of Practice', in Neil Spiller (ed), Δ *Integrating Architecture*, September/October (no 5), 1996, p 119.

Ollie Alsop is a director and founding member of Squint/Opera, a digital media studio with offices in London and New York. He creatively directs a broad mix of digital and interactive content for a diverse range of industries, including the built environment, museums and the emerging green technology sector. He is also responsible for art directing the international animated show for kids, *Messy Goes to OKIDO*. Its mission is to introduce preschool children to the wonders of science. He studied architecture at the Bartlett School of Architecture, University College London (UCL), graduating in 2000.

Thomas Aquilina is a London-based architect and academic dedicated to building communities of radical thought and progressive practice. He is a co-director of the New Architecture Writers programme and a co-founder of publishing collective Afterparti. He holds the Stephen Lawrence Day Foundation Fellowship at the London School of Architecture (LSA) and is an associate lecturer at London Metropolitan University. His ongoing research on Loose-fit Infrastructures explores the everyday life of cities through a synthesis of images and text.

Nigel Coates is an architect, designer, author and academic. His work encompasses buildings, furniture and ideas. His creative process springs from drawing with a characteristically fluid line suggesting movement. Many projects engage with narrative and a reverse archaeology. His ideas were first realised in his many buildings and interiors in Japan, and in the UK with the Geffrye Museum and the Body Zone at the Millennium Dome in London. He exhibited at the Venice Architecture Biennale in 2000, 2006 and 2008. His work features in the collections of the V&A in London, FRAC Centre in Orléans, Tchoban Foundation in Berlin and M+ in Hong Kong.

Sir Peter Cook was a founder of Archigram in the 1960s, taught at the Architectural Association (AA) in London from 1964 to 1990, and was a professor at the Städelschule, Frankfurt, from 1984 to 2009. He was Professor and Chair of the Bartlett School of Architecture, UCL from 1990 to 2006, and is a RIBA Royal Gold Medalist (with Archigram). He has authored nine books, and his drawings are in the collections of the Museum of Modern Art (MoMA) in New York, Deutsches Architekturmuseum (DAM) in Frankfurt, Centre

Pompidou in Paris and FRAC Centre in Orléans. His built works include the Kunsthaus Graz (2003) with Colin Fournier, and with his current practice CRAB studio the departments of Law and Central Administration at the University of Vienna (2013), Abedian School of Architecture at Bond University, Gold Coast, Australia (2014) and the Drawing Studio at the Arts University Bournemouth (2016). He was knighted for services to architecture in 2007. During the pandemic he constructed the Innovation Studio with Tim Culverhouse and has now joined new international practice CHAP (Cook, Haffner Architecture Platform) involved in projects in Asia, the Middle East and Norway. In 2022, a major exhibition of 124 of his drawings was held at the Louisiana Museum in Denmark and the Oslo Triennale.

Paul Finch is Programme Director of the World Architecture Festival (WAF). He has edited *Building Design,* the *Architects' Journal* and *Architectural Review*, where he launched WAF in 2008. He has been co-editor of *Planning in London* since 1994. He was a founder-commissioner and later chair at the Commission for Architecture and the Built Environment (CABE) where he also chaired its design review programme. He chaired CABE's London Olympics design panel from 2005 to 2012. He holds an honorary doctorate from the University of Westminster, London, and honorary fellowships from UCL and the Royal Institute of British Architects (RIBA). He was awarded an OBE for services to architecture in 2002.

Mark Garcia is an academic at the Bartlett School of Architecture and in the Department of the History of Art, UCL. He has held academic posts at the University of Oxford and the Royal College of Art (RCA) in London. He has lectured and exhibited works in Japan, Switzerland, Ireland, Germany and the US. He is the guest-editor of the *AD* issues *Architextiles* (November/December 2006), *Patterns of Architecture* (November/December 2009), *Future Details of Architecture* (July/August 2014) and *Posthuman Architectures* (forthcoming), and editor of the book *The Diagrams of Architecture* (Wiley, 2010). His 2017 solo show 'Up Close' at Cornell University's College of Architecture, Art, and Planning (AAP) in Ithaca, New York, was on the details of Zaha Hadid. His PhD is on the 21st-century posthuman design of spacecraft.

CONTRIBUTORS

Clare Hamman is an architecturally trained designer, documentary producer and consultant interested in the interactions between society, design and representation. Working with universities, small organisations and broadcasters, she is involved in the management and representation of archive collections. Archive material is often central to her projects, whether used to understand the context of the collection itself or presented within the narratives she writes and creates. She has worked on projects including the Archigram Archival Project at the University of Westminster, The Penn Club and the Alsop Collection at the Marco Goldschmied Foundation in London.

John Lyall studied at the AA in London. He is a director of Lyall, Bills & Young Architects. The practice's award-winning buildings include the Goldsmiths Centre in London and several infrastructure projects in the city's Olympic Park, and the Jerwood DanceHouse in Ipswich. He is known also for his urban regeneration work in Leeds, Cardiff Bay, Ipswich Waterfront, and more recently in Chatham, Kent. He worked for Cedric Price and Piano+Rogers before setting up practice with Will Alsop. Their studio produced significant schemes such as rail stations at North Greenwich and Tottenham Hale and the Cardiff Bay Visitor Centre.

Bruce McLean studied at the Glasgow School of Art from 1961 to 1963, and at Saint Martin's School of Art, London, from 1963 to 1966. He has produced paintings, sculptures, ceramics, prints, films, performances, books and buildings. In 1985 he won the John Moores Painting Prize and began teaching at the Slade School of Fine Art in London where he subsequently became Head of Graduate Painting and Professor of Fine Art (2002–10). His work is held in private and public collections including Tate and the V&A in London and the National Museum of Modern Art in Edinburgh.

Will McLean leads the technical teaching across the School of Architecture and Cities at the University of Westminster. He writes about architecture, technology and construction history, and has co-authored five books with colleague Pete Silver, including *Structural Engineering for Architects: A Handbook* (Laurence King, 2014), *Introduction to Architectural Technology* (Laurence King, 2021) and *The Environmental Design Sourcebook* (RIBA Publishing, 2021). In 2008 he established the architectural imprint Bibliotheque McLean, publishing titles including *Sabbioneta: Cryptic City* by James Madge (2011), *Quik Build:*

Adam Kalkin's ABC of Container Architecture (2008) and *Building with Air* (2014) by Dante Bini.

Kester Rattenbury is an architectural writer, teacher and Professor at the University of Westminster where she set up the research group EXP and leads on practice-based research. Her major projects include *This Is Not Architecture* (Routledge, 2002), the Archigram Archival Project (2010), the Supercrit series (publications 2003–12 with Samantha Hardingham) and *The Wessex Project: Thomas Hardy Architect* (Lund Humphries, 2018).

Marcos Rosello is the founding director of aLL Design, which he established with Will Alsop in 2011. He has been pivotal in leading the practice, setting direction and growing both UK domestic and international offices. As a chartered architect with a passion for design, he uses his collective skills to identify and nurture talent, bringing out the best in people, which in turn helps to produce work with a well-thought-through approach to art and design, balancing creativity and commerciality. He enjoys presenting keynote speeches on transformative design that follows the practice's aims of making life better and pushing forward the philosophy of 'knock nothing down'.

Neil Spiller is Editor of $\mathcal{D}$, and was previously Hawksmoor Chair of Architecture and Landscape and Deputy Pro Vice Chancellor at the University of Greenwich in London. Prior to this he was Vice Dean at the Bartlett School of Architecture, UCL. He has made an international reputation as an architect, designer, artist, teacher, writer and polemicist. He is the founding director of the Advanced Virtual and Technological Architecture Research (AVATAR) group, which continues to push the boundaries of architectural design and discourse in the face of the impact of 21st-century technologies. Its current preoccupations include augmented and mixed realities and other metamorphic technologies.

Neil Thomas is the founder and director of innovative engineering practice Atelier One. He holds a number of high-profile academic posts in the UK and US, most recently being a visiting professor at Yale University in New Haven, Connecticut and the Massachusetts Institute of Technology (MIT). In 2014 he was elected Royal Designer for Industry (RDI), an Honorary RIBA Fellowship for his contribution to architecture over the past 25 years, and in 2015 was awarded Fellow of the Institute of Structural Engineers. In 2016 he was honoured with an MBE on the Queen's 90th Birthday for contributions to Architecture, Design and Engineering, and was awarded the Milne Medal in 2019.

What is *Architectural Design*?

Founded in 1930, *Architectural Design* (△) is an influential and prestigious publication. It combines the currency and topicality of a newsstand journal with the rigour and production qualities of a book. With an almost unrivalled reputation worldwide, it is consistently at the forefront of cultural thought and design.

Issues of △ are edited either by the journal Editor, Neil Spiller, or by an invited Guest-Editor. Renowned for being at the leading edge of design and new technologies, △ also covers themes as diverse as architectural history, the environment, interior design, landscape architecture and urban design.

Provocative and pioneering, △ inspires theoretical, creative and technological advances. It questions the outcome of technical innovations as well as the far-reaching social, cultural and environmental challenges that present themselves today.

For further information on △, subscriptions and purchasing single issues see:

https://onlinelibrary.wiley.com/journal/15542769

Volume 91 No 5
ISBN 978 1119 717706

Volume 91 No 6
ISBN 978 1119 812241

Volume 92 No 1
ISBN 978 1119 743255

Volume 92 No 2
ISBN 978 1119 748793

Volume 92 No 3
ISBN 978 1119 748847

Volume 92 No 4
ISBN 978 1119 787778